STRATEGY WORKSHOP
Toolkit

About the Author

The author, Paul Christodoulou, has over 20 years' experience as a strategy leader working in international business based in the UK, USA and France. His early career involved a series of line positions in operations, development and sales, always having a strong role in formulating strategy. He then specialised in running major strategic projects in complex global organisations both as an internal change agent and as an external adviser. His core passion is designing and facilitating strategy projects involving senior teams and using strategy workshops as the key building blocks. He has led over 150 strategy workshops in companies including BAE Systems, Beiersdorf, Blue Circle, BOC, Bombardier, Caterpillar, Douwe Egberts, Huntsman, Grundfos, Invensys, Lafarge, Nestlé, Schneider Electric, Sealed Air, Shell and Wavin delivered in countries all over the world including the UK, the USA, Chile, Denmark, France, Germany, Greece, Holland, the Philippines, Singapore, Spain and Switzerland.

Paul originally studied engineering and management at Durham University and Cambridge University in the UK, and holds an MBA with distinction from INSEAD in France. He founded Strajectory, a strategic advisory company, in 2002 and is also a senior associate at the Cambridge University Institute for Manufacturing.

STRATEGY WORKSHOP
Toolkit

How to 'herd wild cats' and create breakthrough strategies

PAUL CHRISTODOULOU

Illustrations by Lisa Buckley

strajectory

First published in the United Kingdom in 2010 by
Strajectory Books

ISBN 978-0-9565638-0-4

Book Production by The Choir Press

CONTENTS

Acknowledgements

This toolkit is simply a collection of practical techniques and experiences borrowed and developed by the author over a period of 20 years working as a manager and change agent in international business organisations. It is therefore of primary importance to recognise the crucial role and contribution of the various employers, clients, collaborators and colleagues who have been the inspiration for, and the source of, much of the content. Worthy of particular note here are the following mentors and guides: John Lucas and Gary Kedgley of APV Baker; Derek Marshall of BOC; Jonathan Nightingale of Blue Circle; Philippe Gruat of Lafarge; Adrian Harwood of Interbrand; Mike Gregory, Peter Templeton, Phil Hanson and Don Fleet of Cambridge University; Fred Mason and Rod Skewes; Chris Woodbridge and Mike Donoghue of Sealed Air.

FOREWORD

Most people in my walk of life are reluctant to accept that the word 'consultant' best describes what they do. Sadly the word has many unwanted connotations and there are plenty of well-repeated jokes at the expense of consultants. It is, however, an important occupation that needs 'best practice' just like any other profession.

Until I started working with Paul Christodoulou, I knew basically two different ways of going about my task as a consultant. The first was to adopt a role as a sort of 'guru consultant', trading on the years I have been privileged to walk other people's business corridors. It gives you a sort of sixth sense about what can be realistically achieved in the sub-culture of any particular organisation. It tends to play out as a mentoring relationship with the person who engaged you and delivers its change agenda through that person.

The second approach in my kit bag will be very familiar to anyone who has worked for or with the big consulting firms. It hinges on the use of a repeatable methodology. Consulting firms adopt this approach for many reasons. It enables very flexible deployment of people if they are all trained in a common approach. It is a good platform for capturing learning and most of all it is predictable and efficient. The emphasis is on gathering data and then turning the data into findings and the findings into conclusions. The end product is typically a set of recommendations that enjoy a high degree of analytical integrity.

What Paul has shared in this book is a 'third way' for any of us in the business of strategy. I have been fortunate to be part of several of his case study situations and enjoyed first hand the attractions of this collaborative approach which has sometimes been described as 'guided discovery'. As an engineer I have long known that the more people you can involve in the design process the better will be the product. Why then should it be any different when designing strategy? I once had a boss who proudly announced that he alone would do strategy and the rest of us could do 'execution'. The result for me was totally demoralising. We are all motivated to develop strategy. We all have our preferred theories about which way things should go based on the accumulated wisdom of earlier experiences.

What this approach to strategy development does is to liberate all that collective wisdom, to test all those pet theories and to challenge the much-loved conventions that first grew up in earlier and different circumstances. Experience and intuition are mixed with just the right amount of hard data. It gives all the participants in the process the opportunity to stand above their fiefdoms and to take a general's view of the business.

What I have seen as an outcome is strategy formulation that is genuinely breakthrough thinking and which enjoys an incredible level of buy-in from the entire team. It leaves people wanting to be part of the long-term picture. Long after these projects I have bumped into people who are only too pleased to recall the buzz of developing strategy this way.

I am delighted that Paul has taken the time to distil these experiences into such a practical book which will hopefully not just sit on the bookshelf but will be regularly re-explored as an inspiration to trying this collaborative approach to strategy formulation.

Phil Hanson
Former Lead Principal, IBM Consulting

Introducing the wild cats (and other jungle animals)

INTRODUCTION

Modern organisational trends are making it harder than ever to develop winning strategies at the same time as running the everyday business. Empowerment and flatter structures mean that decision-making is more and more dispersed across a complex matrix of semi-autonomous managers. This makes strategic development vulnerable to misalignment and fragmentation. Workshops involving all the senior players are increasingly the medium by which joined-up strategies are forged in leading businesses. But running strategy workshops can often feel like herding wild cats. This book provides a toolkit of tried-and-tested techniques to aid the strategy leader in delivering successful outcomes.

Why team workshops are now central to strategy development

The age of top-down strategy is long gone. Strategy is now more 'middle-up', created by flexible teams of empowered managers via intense, workshop-based initiatives led by inspirational strategy leaders. These staged events are the means by which facts, experience and expert judgement merge. Workshops often require significant preparation and involve structured tools for effectively guiding the multiple talents within the team. The overall strategy process typically extends over several months, involving a sequence of workshops interspersed with detailed analysis. Workshops are critical within this process as the means for inspiring creative breakthroughs, for driving out deliverables, and for ensuring buy-in. When this process is orchestrated effectively, 'planning' merges seamlessly into 'doing' and significant business benefits automatically follow.

Why leading successful strategy workshops isn't easy

The strategy leader is handed something of a poisoned chalice. He or she:
- often has no formal authority, yet needs to corral a group of senior, strong-willed managers to create breakthrough thinking that everyone buys into;
- needs to guide a structured process that involves all the right people while cutting through the politics and satisfying the vested interests;
- has to tap into the gut instincts of those who live-and-breathe the business but also needs to build in an injection of fresh external thinking;
- needs to support the team process with facts and analytical rigour, but without disappearing in a sea of data.

The strategy leader's role sometimes feels like trying to herd wild cats

Strategy Workshop Toolkit

This book aims to provide extensive support to the strategy leader in running the critical workshops that support strategy development in modern organisations. It consists of key principles, structured techniques and practical tips for ensuring successful workshop outcomes. It is based on over 20 years of experience in leading strategy workshops in a range of blue chip businesses. It is intended as a reference guide, not to be read once and discarded, but to be accessed repeatedly over time to aid the planning and execution of strategy workshops that can lead directly to fresh ideas, joined-up thinking, motivated managers and significant business benefits.

A
FIVE STRATEGY SUCCESS STORIES

Overview
Diversification Strategy
Technology Strategy
Global Marketing Strategy
Business Process Re-engineering Strategy
Global Production Strategy

OVERVIEW

In order to ground this guide in reality, and to provide a framework for illustrating the toolkit that follows, a set of five real-life 'strategy success stories' is outlined below and described in the following pages.

	Diversification	Technology	Global Marketing	Business Process Re-engineering	Global Production
Sector	Retail Services	Audio Equipment	Building Materials	Food Machinery	Packaging
Turnover/ # staff	$20m 100 staff	$30m 200 staff	$3bn 10,000 staff	$200m 1,800 staff	$5bn 15,000 staff
Project objective	How to diversify into more profitable sectors	How to develop a 3 year R&D strategy	How to develop global synergies and profit growth	How to transform operational performance	How to optimise the global network of plants
Who was involved	6 senior executives	Cross-functional team of 16	15 regional marketing directors	105 senior executives & managers	110 senior executives & managers
Duration	2 months	3 months	6 weeks	12 months	12 months
Hard benefits	50% growth over 5 years	Defence of premium margins	$15m profits from year 1 growth projects	Enabler to 10% operational savings	$55m annual cost savings by year 5
Soft benefits	Consensus on diversification priorities	Effective use of limited investment	Cross-fertilisation across geographies	Retrained entire workforce in best practice	Total immersion of senior team in change imperative

increasing project complexity →

A broad range of applications

The five case studies are all based on real strategy projects led by the author over the last 20 years. They are deliberately diverse in almost every respect: company size, business sector, functional focus, project duration, numbers of staff involved, and strategic objectives. The stories are introduced one-by-one in this section, and are then referenced repeatedly within this guide to help illustrate the application of the various principles, techniques and practical tips.

DIVERSIFICATION STRATEGY

This first case study is one of the simpler examples used in this guide involving a small company and a small team of senior managers. One key aspect was developing consensus amongst a team of strong individuals while making sure that the CEO could still demonstrate authority (but without dominating).

Sector
Retail services

Products
Checkout equipment (tills etc)

Turnover / # staff
$20m / 100 staff

Project objective
How to diversify the product range and customer base into more profitable sectors

Who was involved
6 senior executives: CEO and functional heads for sales, strategic marketing, engineering, operations and finance

My role
External strategy leader & coach

Project duration
2 months

The burning platform
Breaking away from the 'comfort zone' of a single major account that had historically led strategic development

The story

This small company was a value-added reseller supplying and maintaining checkout equipment used by major supermarkets. The company was profitable but relying too heavily on one very large key account, which was notoriously demanding and tended to suck in any available resources. The major imperative was therefore to develop a diversification strategy in terms of new markets and products to reduce exposure to the major client (while retaining them as a valuable co-development partner).

The company had around 100 staff and an executive board consisting of the CEO plus 5 functional heads. The CEO, previously famously autocratic, wanted to shift to a more consultative approach and wanted more from his senior team.

The project approach balanced collective creativity with individual accountability, and ensured rapid development of a joined-up strategy. The consultative approach ensured consensus and buy-in, with the CEO given some scope to show leadership when consensus could not be reached.

The project was completed in less than 2 months, and led to accelerated growth in new products, services and sectors and increased profitability.

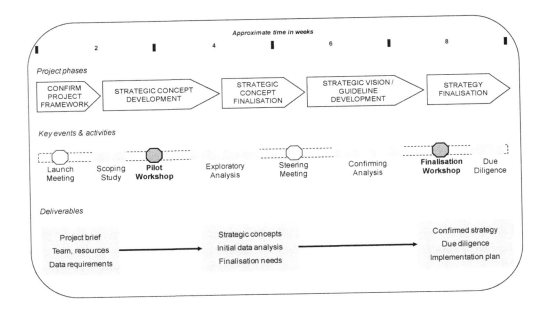

The plan

The project involved five phases covering the framework, concepts, vision, guidelines and finalisation. The activities were organised around two major workshop events involving the executive board. The initial pilot workshop, held over two days, supported the major creative activity. This used straightforward tools for understanding key contextual drivers followed by development and evaluation of strategic options. The output was a set of strategic concepts that then required validating analysis by individual managers and their teams. This background work was progressed intensively in preparation for a one-day finalisation workshop which served to refine and sign off the final strategy.

Hard benefits
50% growth over 5 years from selling existing products into new accounts, and developing new products for existing accounts.

Soft benefits
Consensus amongst team of strong individuals which led to a concerted, joined-up effort to deliver the strategy.

TECHNOLOGY STRATEGY

The second case study involved developing a strategy for new product and service technology for a small, premium hi-fi company. In the past, this had strictly been the domain of the R&D department. Using a broader team in a workshop-based approach ensured more creativity, better and more practical ideas, and quicker time-to-market.

Sector
Specialist audio equipment

Products
Amplifiers, CD players, speakers

Turnover / # staff
$30m / 200 staff

Project objective
How to develop a 3–year technology strategy including product and service development

Who was involved
Cross-functional team of 16 with a mix of senior and middle managers

My role
External strategy leader

Project duration
3 months

The burning platform
How to renew competitive differentiation and protect premium margins.

The story

This project involved a small, specialist audio equipment supplier with around $30m annual turnover and 200 staff. Although the company enjoyed premium margins, this was heavily dependent on maintaining a technical lead on competitors. The aim of the project was to develop a 3–year plan for R&D investment in new product and service offerings to support ongoing differentiation.

One key aspect was to co-ordinate a broader set of inputs covering not just R&D staff but also staff from sales, marketing, production and finance. This included senior managers as well as key middle managers who had depth of experience and strong opinions.

The result was a multi-dimensional development plan including not only new products but also new integrated systems and innovative, internet-based services. This switch to systems and services represented a radical shift in the business model. One particular advantage of using a larger cross-functional team was a significant reduction in time-to-market for the new developments. With all functions involved from the outset, the detailed design, marketing and launch plans progressed rapidly in parallel rather than in sequence.

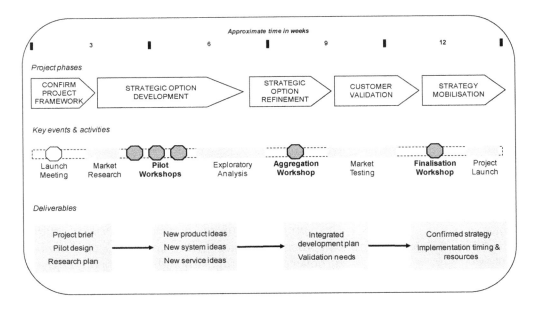

The plan

This project was designed around five major workshops which formed the backbone of the approach. In advance of these, external market research was carried out around customer focus groups. Three separate pilot workshops were then held, each of one day's duration, covering product, system and service development separately. The structure for these creative sessions forced consideration of totally new business models. Following background analysis and development of the key options, an aggregation workshop was held to merge the ideas into a coherent, cross-functional plan. Some market testing (again using customer focus groups) was carried out to refine the ideas before a finalisation workshop where detailed launch plans were devised.

Hard benefits
Reduction in time-to-market for new offerings from 9 months to 4 months. Long-term growth and protection of premium margins.

Soft benefits
Improved creativity and dynamism of the R&D process. Strong motivation in all departments to transform the business.

GLOBAL MARKETING STRATEGY

The third case study was a project undertaken in a large, multi-national company making building materials. The company had just expanded by acquisition then suddenly came under a hostile take-over threat. There was a strong requirement to rapidly increase profits and one mechanism for this was to extract synergies from a globally co-ordinated approach to marketing. This required previously competing local marketing directors to share the secrets of their success – quite a challenge!

Sector
Building materials

Products
Cement, aggregates, concrete

Turnover / # staff
$3bn / 10,000 staff

Project objective
How to develop global synergies & rapid profit improvement (and defeat a hostile take-over bid)

Who was involved
15 regional marketing directors

My role
Global marketing director (and the man from HQ there to help!)

Project duration
6 weeks

The burning platform
To urgently combine the strengths of a diverse set of independent country businesses to raise the share price.

The story

This proud global giant, under a hostile take-over threat, was fighting for its survival as an independent. This led to intense pressure to find short-term ways of boosting the share price. The company had recently expanded by acquisition but was still conducting post-merger integration. One immediate opportunity was the integration of 15 separate regional marketing organisations, each with its strengths and weaknesses. We needed to rapidly identify a strategy with focus on driving quick wins in terms of market growth and profit improvement.

The team included the 15 regional sales and marketing directors, a particularly outgoing and competitive set of wild cats, led by myself as global marketing director with analyst support. We needed to quickly extract the collective wisdom and judgement of the team, supported by pragmatic analysis of external and internal data, and find robust initiatives that could be launched immediately.

The result was an urgent, co-ordinated strategic thrust that delivered $15m of additional annual profits in 1 year. It had taken just 6 weeks to develop and agree this strategy across a diverse global business. The hostile take-over bid was defeated later on in that same year.

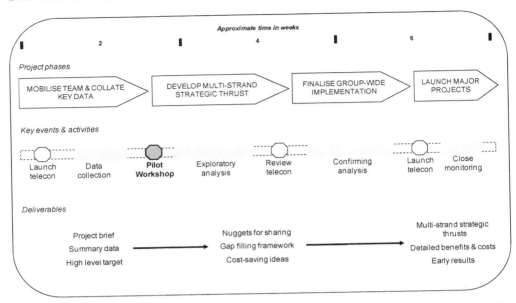

The plan

The format followed a simple, pragmatic framework in line with the urgent nature of the project. This relied on a single intensive workshop activity held over two days. The cost of flying marketing directors from five continents to a hotel at Heathrow airport was significant but the face-to-face contact was crucial for building trust and for inspiring creativity. Key data was prepared in advance of the workshop, after which 'champions' for various group-wide initiatives were tasked with driving ongoing analysis to confirm details and cost–benefit justification. Two teleconference events were then used to drive progress culminating in the launch of specific strategic initiatives with immediate tangible results.

Hard benefits	Soft benefits
$15m profit growth in 1 year from specific short-sharp projects.	Priming of global peer group for ongoing sharing of best practice and co-ordinated strategy development.

BUSINESS PROCESS RE-ENGINEERING STRATEGY

The penultimate case study was undertaken in a multi-national company which designed and manufactured bespoke food production lines. This was a multi-faceted, business process re-engineering challenge which aimed to radically change the culture and ways of working, and just happened to be enabled by a jump to latest business systems. It was a kind of 'big bang' step into a brave new world of global integration.

Sector
Food machinery

Products
Mixers, moulders, ovens, chocolate coating machines

Turnover / # staff
$200m / 1,800 staff

Project objective
How to transform operational performance via new working practices and systems

Who was involved
105 senior executives, middle managers and functional experts

My role
Full-time strategy leader

Project duration
12 months

The burning platform
To use global scale as a competitive weapon against small, low-cost specialists who were cherry-picking the attractive business segments.

The story

This project was conducted in a mid-sized global company which was under severe pressure from small, local competitors. It enjoyed greater global reach than these aggressive, low-cost outfits and, being involved in complex, bespoke engineering, saw an opportunity to make better use of its global pool of resources. The project involved redefining the business processes, replacing all the business systems, and retraining the entire workforce – all in a hectic 12–month period.

The initiative inspired the whole organisation to develop and implement enhanced ways of working which directly led to better designed products, reduced costs, and improved customer lead-times. This involved complete overhaul of the business procedures, and redefinition of responsibilities in, and across, the global matrix structure. It also immersed the whole organisation into a cultural change which embodied the principles of empowerment and continuous improvement.

Over 100 managers were involved in designing the strategy, and 1,800 staff were retrained in better ways of working across Europe, the Americas and Asia-Pacific. Within 2 years, the erosion of market share to low-cost competitors had been overturned by offering better products cheaper and faster.

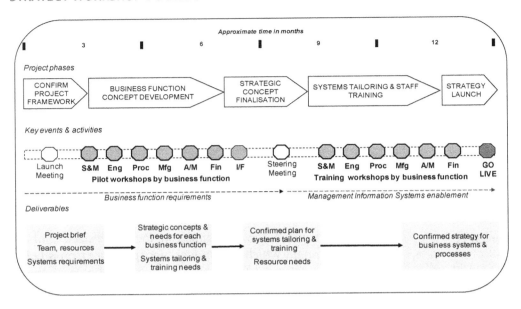

The plan

This project followed the principle of disaggregating the problem around the appropriate organisational structures. The starting point was to run identical workshops for each of the six main business functions to determine the strategic concepts for operational improvement within each. A seventh workshop was added involving a cross-functional team to cover the interfaces. These concepts were then used to finalise the detailed BPR strategy which was institutionalised via a series of training workshops by function on a global basis. The project culminated in a formal 'big bang' style start-up of new business systems.

Hard benefits
Led to 10% costs savings, reduction in typical cycle-times from 12 to 8 weeks, and reversed a long-term decline in sales and profits.

Soft benefits
This created, for the first time, a truly global organisation with common products, production platforms, branding and working practices.

GLOBAL PRODUCTION STRATEGY

The final case study involves a global leader in packaging which needed to transform its production footprint. The company had historically been managed at a local country and region level. Expansion by acquisition meant that there was tremendous opportunity to optimise an asset footprint comprising over 80 production plants somewhat haphazardly spread across the globe. Inspiring a global view, and getting away from parochial local attitudes, was one of the major challenges. The project led to a $250m restructuring programme which exceeded all expectations and helped the company to re-establish cost, market and technology advantages over competitors.

Sector
Packaging

Products
Hi-tech plastic packaging

Turnover / # staff
$5bn / 15,000 staff

Project objective
How to optimise a global network of plants following serial M&A

Who was involved
110 executives and managers covering 4 global product lines and 3 regional businesses

My role
Led a team of four strategy leaders

Project duration
12 months

The burning platform
To radically reduce cost and expand access to new markets

The story

This $5bn global leader had grown significantly by acquisition over the preceding 10 years leaving a large number of production facilities around the world that did not really make sense as an ongoing network. The imperative was to develop a global production strategy that would optimise the plant network to reduce cost and provide a platform for growth in the major emerging markets.

This is a good example of a major project in a complex matrix organisation. This was made up of 3 autonomous regional businesses (Americas, Europe, Asia) which needed to be optimised across 4 global product lines. The dynamics and tensions within the complex matrix of responsibilities was a key feature of the project. The strategy development process involved 110 senior 'wild cats' and took around 12 months. This process created a radical new way of managing not just production but the whole global business. It created an organisation that was truly both global and local, and provided the blueprint for a $250m transformation programme. 5 years on, the project had created $55m in repeating annual savings for the company as well as new market leading positions in Asia, South America and Eastern Europe.

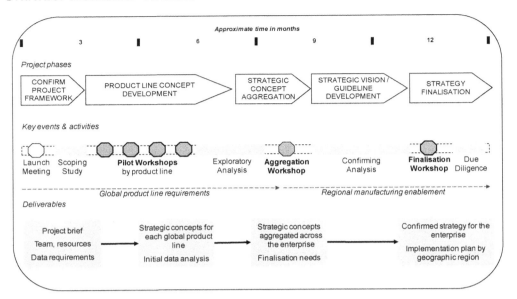

The plan

This project required the development of strategies across a matrix of global product lines and geographic regions. The format was therefore built around pilot workshops for each global product line followed by an aggregation workshop where the emphasis was switched to region. This aligned perfectly with presenting the product lines as project 'customers' and the regions as 'suppliers'. After the strategic framework was created, a great deal of fine-tuning and financial analysis was required to support a major board proposal (including a rights issue to finance the restructuring). During this phase, a finalisation workshop was held to formalise the strategy and to agree mobilisation plans.

Hard benefits
$55m repeating annual cost savings by Year 5. Led to leading positions in major emerging markets. Reinvigoration of process technology leadership.

Soft benefits
Total immersion of senior team in the urgent need to change. An organisation that was both global and local.

B
SIXTEEN GOLDEN RULES

Overview
Plan a Journey of Discovery
Herd the Wild Cats
Create a Burning Platform
Secure Executive Sponsorship
Get Everyone on the Same Page
Structure the Team
Use Consultants Wisely
Engage the Team
Predict Winners and Losers
Blend Experience, Gut-feel and Facts
Find the Right Level of Data
Estimate the Size-of-the-Prize
Exploit the Organisational Dynamics
Expose the Breakthrough Point
Define How to Make it Happen
Move from Planning to Doing

OVERVIEW

As demonstrated by the case studies in the previous section, there is a lot more to developing strategy than just running a few workshops. The workshops are the vehicles for collective creativity, directional decisions, and motivating the team. But these need to be set in a broader project context. This section describes a set of 'golden rules' regarding how to run strategy workshops in this wider context, presented in rough chronological sequence as they apply within the strategy project lifecycle. The 'golden rules' cover a mix of themes including overall project design, the role of analysis, and managing organisational behaviour as outlined below.

Overall project design

Strategy workshops are ineffective if they are not set within a broader project context. The overall strategy project requires careful design to cover complementary activities in preparing for these critical team events, and in post-processing the outputs. This approach should be seen as a 'structured journey of discovery' where the workshops form important milestones.

The role of analysis

Strategy workshops alone will not deliver a fully robust, data-supported business plan as there is only so much detail that can be covered in these intense, group activities. The project plan needs to cover complementary activities including detailed preparation of useful data in advance of workshops, and detailed analysis of 'working proposition' strategies following workshops.

Managing organisational behaviour

Several of the 'golden rules' presented in this section provide guidance on how to manage strategy workshops within complex organisational cultures i.e. the challenges of 'herding wild cats'. This slightly irreverent, fun theme is used to illustrate some very serious principles regarding how to manage and motivate a team of strong-minded, influential individuals.

Rule 1 – PLAN A JOURNEY OF DISCOVERY

Developing strategy should be a structured 'journey of discovery' for the project team. Designing the journey is the first crucial task. There are natural phases and milestones in the journey, and different types of activities to ensure the right blend of experience, gut-feel and facts. Team workshops typically form the backbone, with supporting analysis filling out the flesh. The project needs to start with divergent, creative thinking and move steadily towards more convergent, analytical thinking.

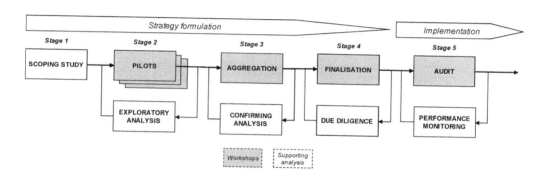

A typical project plan

The diagram above illustrates a typical approach in terms of five sequential stages involving a mix of workshop activities and supporting analysis. The aim of the workshops is to liberate the combined experience and judgement of the management team as the basis for formulating the strategy. The supporting analysis is used for further exploration and validation of the various strategic elements. Getting the right balance between expert judgement and analysis is a critical aspect of this guided journey. This approach places the 'accumulated wisdom' of the management team at the centre of strategy-making while respecting the value of unemotional factual analysis. It involves cycles of experimentation and evaluation to enable innovative thinking to develop and mature. The various stages are described in outline below.

		Key Tasks by Project Stage
1	**Scoping Study**	o Collect background data about the context to the project. o Engage the project team via a structured consultation process. o Test for political hot-spots. o Assess the profiles and motivations of the key players.
2	**Pilots & Exploratory Analysis**	o Run multiple pilot workshops to break a complex strategic challenge into a set of smaller, more manageable topics. o Ensure each pilot workshop involves structured activities for creativity and evaluation leading to a strategy 'working proposition' for that topic area. o Conduct exploratory analysis after each pilot workshop to test and refine these 'working propositions' in preparation for the next project stage.
3	**Aggregation & Confirming Analysis**	o Run an aggregation workshop to combine the results from the pilot studies into a set of common strategic principles. o Identify common themes and interfaces, and design a 'new language'. o Create a first-draft definition of the desired strategic end-state. o Create a first-draft implementation plan. o Conduct confirming analysis to refine the various strategic elements.
4	**Finalisation & Due Diligence**	o Run a finalisation workshop to formalise the detailed strategy and implementation plans against full financial and risk analysis. o Define and launch the 'foundation' projects that collectively ensure the realisation of the future vision. o Define a complementary set of 'enabling' projects covering cross-cutting themes such as communications, finance and legal services. o Agree the key accountabilities and performance targets with the implementation team. o Conduct formal due diligence if required to satisfy external stakeholders.
5	**Audit & Performance Monitoring**	o Conduct a formalised audit of the early experiences of project implementation. o Involve the key implementation champions in sharing early experiences and learnings. o Adjust the strategy accordingly to ensure ongoing effectiveness and practicality. o Formally hand over to the implementation team.

Practical Tips – Planning a Structured Journey of Discovery

1 — *Involve all stakeholders at the outset to agree the project framework*
This is ideally via individual face-to-face or telephone discussions against a simple project brief. It helps to engage the stakeholders but also informs the strategy leader of the range of pet theories and political tensions.

2 — *Use workshops as focal points for creating and agreeing strategy*
Workshops are where experience, gut-feel and facts come together in a creative and meaningful way. They are also key events for building ownership and motivation.

3 — *Use regular telephone meetings for project updates, not for workshops*
Telephone or video conference meetings work especially well to support communications in projects that cross continents and time zones. They do not work well for intense workshop activities where face-to-face contact is critical for building common understanding and for working through the politics.

4 — *Design the process to involve divergent then convergent thinking*
The first challenge is to develop a range of possible strategic concepts via creative, divergent thinking. These concepts then need to converge on clear conclusions and finalised guidelines using more analytical methods.

5 — *Design the project to fit the project customer–supplier relationships*
Each project has its own unique relationships which directly support the objectives. As a general rule, pilot workshops should help define customer requirements and aggregation/ finalisation workshops should help confirm how suppliers will meet these.

6 — *Hold pilot workshops early on in the process*
The earlier the better regarding when to involve key stakeholders in forming the strategic concepts via pilot workshops. Liberating the accumulated wisdom is a great starting point and helps to guide the exploratory analysis. Data analysis without a guiding structure of informed thinking lacks direction and is inefficient.

7 — *Use pilot workshops to crystallise the strategy 'working proposition'*
The pilot workshops should ideally go as far as developing a 'hypothesis' for the key elements of the strategy. This will change as the supporting analysis becomes more mature but making an educated guess early on provides a focus for the ongoing efforts.

8 — *Do not apply formal analysis until after the strategic concepts are clear*
It is tempting to resort to formal financial analysis straight away as this gives an air of credibility. However, this can substitute for developing clear strategic concepts and principles which should be the first priority.

9 — *Use the finalisation workshop to sign off the strategy and mobilise launch*
This event is typically less creative and more confirmatory. Its role is to get agreement to the plan and to energise mobilisation.

CASE STUDY – **Business Process Re-engineering Strategy**

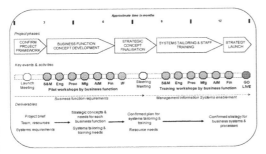

The *BPR Strategy* case study is a good example of a complex, tailored project format designed as a 'structured journey of discovery'. This approach followed the principle of disaggregating the problem around the appropriate organisational structures. Here the central aim was to improve functional operational performance uniformly across a large global business (but ensuring that interfaces between functions were also improved). The starting point was to run identical workshops for each of the six main business functions to determine the strategic concepts for operational improvement within each. A seventh workshop was added involving a cross-functional team to cover the interfaces. These concepts were then used to finalise the detailed BPR Strategy which was then institutionalised via new tailored business systems and a series of training workshops by function on a global basis. These training workshops further tested and fine tuned the operational procedures involving ongoing tailoring of the business systems software.

This structured journey of discovery proved an extremely powerful way to immerse the whole organisation in developing and implementing enhanced business processes with significant benefits in operational efficiencies and responsiveness. Underlying the project format was a similar internal customer–supplier dynamic to the previous example. Here the business functions were positioned as internal customers, and the management information systems department as the internal supplier. The outcome was a radical re-engineering of the global business to deliver better designed products more efficiently in significantly reduced timescales. This involved complete replacement of the business systems, documentation of new business procedures, and clarification of responsibilities in and across the global matrix structure. It also immersed the whole organisation into a cultural change which embodied the principles of empowerment and continuous improvement. Over 100 managers were involved in designing the strategy, and 1,800 staff were retrained in better ways of working.

Rule 2 – HERD THE WILD CATS

The trouble with strategy projects and workshops is that you do not have the luxury of building a balanced team profile of the type that the Belbin theory on team roles would recommend. By definition, this process artificially rounds up opinion-leaders who come with strong egos and individual agendas. The risk of chaos and conflict is high, but the benefits from effectively channelling this wealth of ability and experience are much higher. Here are some guidelines for herding the wild cats and harnessing their collective powers.

The Wild Cats

| **Lion** | **Cheetah** | **Tiger** | **Panther** | **Leopard** |
| Project Sponsor | Pace Setter | Enforcer | Politician | Avoider |

Other Jungle Animals

| **Wild Dog** | **Hyena** | **Antelope** |
| Strategy Leader | Corporate Influencer | Project Analyst |

The wild cats (and other jungle animals)

The aim here is to characterise the different psychological profiles that exist in the modern 'jungle' of strategy projects, and to mould project roles and contributions to fit. The 'wild cats' analogy is used to create a framework of profile types that often emerge during strategic projects. This takes a light-hearted view on the peculiarities of organisational and individual behaviour.

The Wild Cats	
Lion Project Sponsor	The lion is the project sponsor – the king of this contrived jungle. In small businesses, this is usually the CEO. In large organisations, this is typically the executive board member with responsibility for the key topic in question. The lion is vital for getting everyone engaged – for persuading them that the project is important and worthy of their attention and efforts. Sponsorship needs to be visible and continuous or the project will falter at the first hurdle. The strategy leader needs to delegate upwards to make the lion roar whenever required.
Tiger Enforcer	Of the other big cats, the tiger is first among equals, known for its strength and prowess. It will often be the most experienced and respected big cat in the room, and others will look to the tiger for leadership. The tiger is usually a strong ally for the strategy leader and can help negotiate through any political stalemates. Regular consultation with the tiger, in public and private, is important to understand the emerging sentiments and under-currents. Bear in mind that it is obviously important not to get on the wrong side of a tiger.
Cheetah Pace Setter	The cheetah is the quickest big cat off the blocks in engaging with the project and in looking to create value. This can be a useful role model, stirring the competitive juices of the other cats and raising levels of ambition. However, cheetah's energy and ambition may cause the other big cats to become defensive and less co-operative. Another concern with the cheetah is that it can lack stamina for prolonged, intensive activity. The strategy leader may feel it necessary to restrain the cheetah in the early stages to ensure team harmony and to conserve cheetah's energy.
Panther Politician	The panther is the sleek, attractive politician of the team and is mostly active out of sight or in the hours of darkness. Panther will spend a lot of time in private one-to-one discussions with lion and tiger, and may even be in regular contact with higher level executives in an attempt to win additional influence. The panther can be a dangerous cat and is not to be under-estimated. Panthers are normally easy to spot – they have a naturally closed style, are intensely protective of their territory, and will typically observe more than they contribute. They often set a negative tone and focus on barriers and problems. The most effective approach is to expose panther tactics and bring them into the open. A panther faced by a collective of other wild cats is normally forced to co-operate.
Leopard Avoider	The leopard is the other difficult animal in the project jungle in that it is simply rarely seen i.e. is good at avoiding all project activities and therefore conveniently avoiding any responsibility. Later on in the project this makes it able to disown any outcomes as it was not properly consulted. Leopard is extremely good at being unavailable to attend vital workshop activities at the last moment. Leopard may send a passive deputy to observe and feed back possible threats by mobile phone in breaks. The only way to get leopard on board is to make it clear that there is more to lose through absence than through direct participation.

Other Jungle Animals	
Wild Dog *Strategy* *Leader*	The strategy leader's role itself as wild dog is important to understand as part of the jungle dynamic. Wild dog's key attributes are dynamism, tenacity and loyalty. Constant high energy is required to win the willing participation of the big cats (who would all rather be out hunting than indulging in frustrating discussions about how to make a better future for the jungle). Unyielding tenacity is required of wild dog when agreements require brokering or when violent clashes are to be moderated. But ultimately wild dog needs to be loyal to the project cause, seeing past the factions to the needs of the whole. Wild dog must also understand its own limitations. While it is built to endure the extended intense activity of a major project, it does not possess the raw strength and power of the big cats and is unlikely to survive any head-on clashes.
Hyena *Corporate* *Influencer*	Hyena is typically a senior corporate influencer who has no line authority. This could be the strategy director, or, in a large matrix organisation, a head office functional role such as global operations, technology or marketing. Hyena could also be a senior external consultant. Hyena's main purpose in life is as a corporate scavenger but in the very positive sense of creating value through increasing efficiency or transferring good practice. However, hyena is often not respected by the big cats. They pride themselves in being the primary predators who hunt and make kills by winning business and making profits. Hyena is seen as a whining and unglamorous bureaucrat, high cost and undeservedly close to the centre of power. But hyenas are also very intelligent and powerful, and in pairs can easily overcome a big cat. Hyena can be a useful ally for the strategy leader in negotiating the big cat politics. However, too close an association may label the strategy leader as just another bureaucrat.
Antelope *Project Analyst*	The antelope as project analyst is the honest broker in the jungle. The role of antelope is neutral to the competing interests of the various big cats and loyalty lies with the project. Antelope needs to be quick thinking and fast-moving, ahead of the game in predicting key data needs that will cut through emotion and wild cat politics. Antelope generally tries to hide away unnoticed and is careful to only make contributions that add real value. Too much visibility, or poorly judged contributions, can result in antelope being eaten for breakfast.

	Practical Tips – Herding Wild Cats
10	**Each cat has a unique natural environment where it feels at ease** Each wild cat on the team will have its strengths and weaknesses, comfort zones and places where it feels threatened. It is the strategy leader's role to understand these, to make the best of the collective strengths, and to predict and prepare for any threatening situations.
11	**Let the big cats regularly run free but don't cause a cat fight** This presents a very tricky dilemma for the strategy leader requiring fine judgement. Fundamental to the strategy process is the need to tap the wisdom and power of these big beasts. But most big cats will naturally try to dominate a group and swing big decisions in its favour. The strategy leader needs to unleash the power but also harness it where necessary.
12	**Big cats need regular feeding with raw meat** Senior business leaders will only properly engage with strategy projects if they can see something in it for them as well as for the greater good. This means providing the prospect of real meat in terms of improved business prospects, better organisational support, lower costs etc. Exactly where the meat is and how they will get it needs to be pointed out to each cat individually by the strategy leader.
13	**Understand potential winners and losers early on and take action** In reality there will always be an uneven mix of benefits from a project, and some business leaders may even emerge worse off. This balance needs to be predicted right from the outset and measures taken to make this worth the effort, even for the losers. This may even require changes to individual remuneration terms or career prospects to compensate. Excluding potential losers from the process is a last resort and will need other resolving actions later on as this only delays a fundamental problem.
14	**Night time activities (i.e. in the bar) often disperse tensions** Time over dinner and in the bar is often a crucial part of intense strategy workshop activities – not just to let off steam but for more informal discussion around key political issues and stalemates. It is always surprising how tensions that were seemingly life-threatening during the day can suddenly dissipate overnight.
15	**Take appropriate action to dissipate continuing tensions** It is the strategy leader's responsibility to spot simmering tensions between individual wild cats and to broker resolution via sensitive intervention. This might mean a discussion in a quiet corner during a break or, as mentioned, later in the bar.

TOP TIP

Create a sense of competition between the big cats on the team by showing how visible their contributions will be to the CEO.

Rule 3 – CREATE A BURNING PLATFORM

Launching the project involves building a sense of urgency – the so-called 'burning platform'. The term originates from the oil industry (i.e. a burning off-shore oil platform) and refers to the urgent need to move from an uncomfortable position. In business terms, this must articulate exactly why we need to change in a simple and compelling fashion. Without it, time-starved managers will not be motivated to get involved.

The strategy leader needs to instil a sense of urgency

How to formulate a burning platform

The typical burning platform sounds like a marketing campaign with a problem statement followed by a value proposition. Examples from the case studies are shown over the page. The marketing analogy is fitting – this needs crisp messages, a communications strategy – even clear branding – to get the interest and involvement of the key players. Some key elements to consider are:

- o Describe a problem statement in terms of external pressures (customer, competitor, technology etc).
- o Paint a troubling picture of what may happen if we do nothing.
- o Quantify the business impact of failure, success or both.
- o Describe what we need to do to put things right.

CASE STUDY – **Global Production Strategy**

THE BURNING PLATFORM

- o We expect powerful supermarkets to impose 1% annual price erosion.
- o We expect powerful petrochem suppliers to impose a 2% annual material cost increase.
- o If we do nothing, our gross margins will halve in 5 years.
- o Lean processes will only deliver 30% of the savings necessary to support today's margins.
- o We must radically change our global production footprint to generate the remaining 70%.

CASE STUDY – **Business Process Re-engineering Strategy**

THE BURNING PLATFORM

- o Small, agile, low-cost competitors are increasingly threatening our dominant market share.
- o As our volumes reduce on a high fixed-cost infrastructure, our business becomes increasingly unsustainable.
- o Our main advantage over the low-cost competitors is our global scale. We must exploit this to create more innovative products and an optimised, seamless supply chain.
- o This requires the complete, radical overhaul of our business processes and systems to make a step change in performance.

TOP TIP
Create a hypothetical Profit and Loss statement 5 years on, painting a gloomy picture of how the business may perform if we do nothing.

Rule 4 – SECURE EXECUTIVE SPONSORSHIP

You may ask why executive sponsorship is required at all in the modern, decentralised, empowered organisation. Surely each business manager and functional head is now fully 'incentivised' and accountable and should be left to deliver or face the 'consequences'. The problem here is that most major strategies need to cross these somewhat arbitrary boundaries in the corporate structure. They require that these quasi-autonomous managers co-operate and collaborate for the greater good. For this to happen, the executive board needs to make the project one of the three or four most important things for the business.

'Middle-up' strategy requires executive sponsorship

Strategy is not a top-down process any more. This used to fit with the old-style hierarchical structures where 'chiefs' decided on priorities and 'indians' followed instructions handed down. In the modern, flat, empowered organisations, strategic initiatives are more likely to be spawned in the middle layers of the organisation. Some of these will be short-lived – either they will be high return/low effort and will just happen without need for intervention, or they will be poorly conceived and will naturally die. The problem with the small number of really important strategic initiatives is that they imply too much disruption to the status quo to happen by themselves, and you cannot afford to let them die. These are the special circumstances when executive sponsorship is required – the big ticket strategic requirements that will not happen by themselves.

How to win executive sponsorship

There are no special secrets for how a strategy leader can gain executive sponsorship. It comes down to determined lobbying and influencing at peer level and at all levels up to the CEO. The strategy leader then needs to make sure that sponsorship from the top is clearly visible. One key consideration is to have the executive sponsor visibly supportive at major workshop events. For all of the case studies described, the CEO provided a brief at the start of the major strategy workshops – either in person or by teleconference – and was often present again towards the end of each session to check on progress. The messages need to be clear and consistent – this project is of primary importance and doing nothing is not an option.

Rule 5 – GET EVERYONE ON THE SAME PAGE

When a major strategy project is launched, it is amazing how quickly key participants develop different ideas of what it is all about. Some will want this to fix their own pet problems, some will have wildly over-ambitious views of what this can achieve, others will just get the wrong end of the stick. Creating a project charter is a way to get everyone (literally) on the same page as they become engaged. This may be a written document or, more likely, a short PowerPoint presentation to guide a personal briefing.

	What a project charter should include
Objectives	o What the project aims to achieve o Some measures of success and broad targets
Burning platform	o Why this is important o What might happen if we don't do this
Scope	o What business areas does this cover? o What areas does it not cover?
Deliverables	o Templates for what the result might look like
Team	o Who is involved and in what capacity o The sponsorship and steering mechanism
Plan & timescales	o The structured journey of discovery o Key milestones with approximate timings o Key dates for workshops and other group activities
Immediate tasks	o What we need to do now o What we need to do next
FAQ	o Prediction of key questions that participants are likely to ask

Rule 6 – STRUCTURE THE TEAM

Building the right team is critical to the success of the modern, consultative approach to strategy. Firstly, you need to access those key individuals that embody the collective wisdom. Secondly, you need the people who have the capability and authority to make it happen. This section describes how to structure the team and how to design individual roles including the core team, key contributors and the steering group.

Steering Group

Executive board	Project sponsor

Key Contributors

Business unit leaders	Functional leaders
Regional leaders	Wise old heads
Rising stars	Key influencers

Core Team

Project leader	Analysts
Admin	Champions

Core Team

The core team is the dedicated project management resource and consists of the strategy leader, financial analysts, admin support and 'champions'. The strategy leader is typically an energetic manager who is destined for very senior roles. The project is a means of rapid career progression: making senior contacts in all parts of the organisation and understanding how every area works. Analysts, probably seconded from the finance function, are an essential support to the strategy leader and should be involved from the outset. Effective admin support is a critical aspect: getting space in everyone's diaries for the fundamental team activities often determines the pace of the project. A first class administrator is worth his/her weight in gold. Appointing a set of 'champions' to the core team – i.e. change agents who will be crucial to the implementation phase – is an important task. Seeding these champions into the process at the start will ultimately support the seamless transition from 'planning' to 'doing'.

Key Contributors

The key contributors are the life-blood of strategy-making. Their contribution covers experience, opinions, judgement and pet theories (and, of course, is naturally accompanied by emotion, politics and individual agendas). This team normally involves a mix of senior and middle managers covering all the affected business areas, regions and functions. There are no fixed rules on the right level of seniority. What is more important is to achieve a good balance on a number of different levels: big-picture thinkers and detailed thinkers, optimists and pessimists, planners and doers, wise old heads and rising stars. The wise old heads are particularly important. This refers to those key individuals who have long, loyal service, and who have relatively modest career aspirations. These individuals often embody the hidden intellectual property of the company, are usually beyond the politics and can act as the 'organisational conscience'. The key contributors are intimately involved in the core workshop activities as well as the various analysis activities outside workshops.

Steering Group

The steering group is typically made up of part or all of the executive board of the company. This has the normal project governance and decision-making role. One important aspect is to make sure that there is some degree of overlap between steering group and key contributors (certainly the executive project sponsor plus maybe one other executive).

Degree of Involvement			
Strategy leader	**Other core team**	**Key contributors**	**Steering group**
Major projects 100% Minor projects 30–50%	Early stages 20–50% Later stages 50–100%	Workshops 100% Otherwise 10–20%	Bi-monthly or quarterly reviews

Rule 7 – USE CONSULTANTS WISELY

There are benefits and risks of using external consultants in major strategy projects. The major benefits include the injection of outside expertise and relevant experience. One major risk is that over-use of consultants can by-pass the accumulated wisdom of the management team and undermine the empowerment and accountability principles. Careful consideration is required regarding how and when to employ outside help.

Important reasons for engaging consultants

o   Having some external input is often essential to freshen the team dynamic and ensure that the thinking does not become parochial or blinkered.
o   External consultants are often able to ask the big, provocative questions that internal politics keeps under covers.
o   It often helps to have external facilitators in the major workshop activities to provide an independent, honest broker role.
o   Consultants who have experience of similar initiatives in other companies can help you to avoid the mistakes others have made.

Key problems to avoid

o   Do not 'outsource' the problem to consultants. Your own management team know the business better than anyone and their experience and intuition is essential to creating breakthrough thinking.
o   Do not use consultants in favour of your own high potential young managers. Investment you make in consultants is enjoyed by their next client. Investment in your own people has ongoing returns for you.
o   Consultants tend to like repeatable, analysis-based methodologies because they are scalable. Do not allow this to limit the vision of your strategic thinking.

TOP TIP
Choose consultants who will do the project **with you** not **to you**.

Rule 8 – ENGAGE THE TEAM

One of the important early activities in major strategy projects is to engage each member of the project team. There are several aims. Firstly, this is a good vehicle for properly briefing each individual on the scope and aims of the project, and to start motivating them to actively take part. Secondly, this is a great opportunity for the strategy leader to start tapping the accumulated wisdom of the key contributors. Last, and by no means least, this provides a unique one-to-one dialogue where the strategy leader can 'test the temperature' regarding any key political or emotive issues at play.

	Practical Tips – Engaging the Team via One-on-One Interviews
16	**Talk to each key contributor individually before the main team activities** This will help you to understand the historic context to the project, and will reveal the key political and personal issues in a safe environment.
17	**Use telephone interviews for efficiency and intimacy** Strangely, telephone interviews tend to work better than face-to-face. Somehow the atmosphere is more intimate and the interviewee feels more able to reveal concerns and personal issues. Also, for a large, multi-site business, telephone discussions are significantly easier logistically to co-ordinate.
18	**45 minutes per interview is about right** This is enough to cover a lot of ground, but not so long that it gets stale.
19	**Use a short checklist of broad topics and an open questioning style** The buzz term is 'active listening'. This means broad questions and leaving plenty of space for the interviewee to fill. But don't go too far. The interview needs to have structure and purpose and you need to keep it on track.
20	**Find out what the interviewee thinks is important** This goes alongside the open style. Leading the discussion too much will limit the content to what you think is important. You really want to know what the interviewee thinks is important.
21	**Air time should be 80% interviewee, 20% interviewer** Consider recording the first interview to check back whether you are talking too much.
22	**Circulate a summarised, anonymous digest of the key interview findings** This provides an excellent orientation map for the whole project team. Use this as an opportunity to air any obvious concerns or hot political issues raised (but keep all the references anonymous).

Rule 9 – PREDICT WINNERS AND LOSERS

As soon as the project is launched and the team engaged, the likely winners and losers will become apparent. The problem is that at least some of the big potential losers will be on the team that is shaping the strategy and, as the saying goes, turkeys rarely vote for Christmas. The strategy leader needs to be considering this right from the project inception as this can create a negative influence or even de-rail the project completely.

Exclude potential losers or take a more proactive approach?

In many cases, companies cope with this by excluding obvious potential losers from the strategy development process. This is effective in avoiding a sticky short-term problem, but it may just delay the pain or even increase the potential disruption when the news of the project inevitably leaks. This approach also goes against the key principles of empowerment and accountability that this consultative strategy process is designed to support. It may also exclude important expertise and experience. Ideally this needs a more considered and creative approach which redefines the roles of individuals and aligns incentives to fit with the project objectives.

CASE STUDY – Aligning roles and incentives

A good example arose in the *Global Production Strategy* case study concerning one of the key project contributors who was Production Director for the US with responsibility for six large factories. This individual had 20 years' service starting as an engineering graduate and then building a wealth of accumulated wisdom. This was accompanied, as you might expect, with a strong emotional attachment and a proudly defensive attitude. The looming prospect of moving some of his workload to lower-cost sites in Mexico felt like an aggressive attack on his close family. This senior manager's response was to resist change at any cost. The creative solution was to redefine his role to cover all of the North America production operations including Mexico, an effective promotion accompanied with status and financial benefits. The hard reality of the situation needed to be communicated to support the transition i.e. 'this change is going to happen anyway and it's your choice whether you want to help make it happen in the best possible way or whether you want to be excluded'. In this sense, many individual roles may change through the course of a major change project. This transition in individual roles and incentives needs to be planned and facilitated by the strategy leader.

Rule 10 – BLEND EXPERIENCE, GUT-FEEL AND FACTS

Developing innovative strategy requires a balance of 'hard' data analysis and 'softer' inputs such as the collective wisdom and experience of the management team. Many organisations go to one or other extreme. Intensive strategy workshops are the perfect means for combining hard and soft inputs in a balanced way.

Workshops are the perfect vehicle for blending experience, gut-feel and facts

Why workshops are crucial for effective strategy-making

Strategy workshops are ideally suited to bringing data analysis, collective experience, and gut-feel all together at the same time. A well-designed and well-run workshop allows creative freedom but always informed with meaningful data. Gut-feel instincts can be tapped but can also be tested and evaluated against objective analytical frameworks. And often it is the sharing of ideas based on facts, the sound-boarding between different workshop participants, and the building on each other's theories that inspires the truly novel thinking and the deeper understanding of the fundamental drivers and principles.

CASE STUDY – ## Global Marketing Strategy

The *Global Marketing Strategy* case study is a simple vehicle for illustrating this point. To recap, this global building materials giant was under hostile take-over threat and therefore under considerable pressure to find short-term ways of boosting the share price. The company had recently expanded by acquisition but was still conducting post-merger integration. One immediate opportunity was the integration of 15 separate regional marketing organisations which each had strengths and weaknesses. This meant rapidly identifying an integration strategy with focus on driving quick wins in terms of market growth and profit improvement.

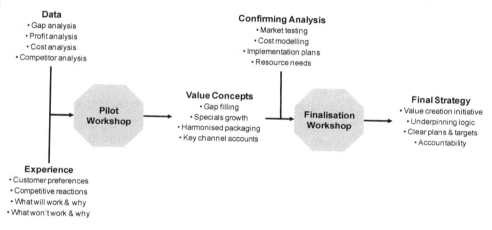

Data
- Gap analysis
- Profit analysis
- Cost analysis
- Competitor analysis

Confirming Analysis
- Market testing
- Cost modelling
- Implementation plans
- Resource needs

Pilot Workshop

Value Concepts
- Gap filling
- Specials growth
- Harmonised packaging
- Key channel accounts

Finalisation Workshop

Final Strategy
- Value creation initiative
- Underpinning logic
- Clear plans & targets
- Accountability

Experience
- Customer preferences
- Competitive reactions
- What will work & why
- What won't work & why

The diagram above illustrates the use of workshops to blend the experience of the team with an appropriate level of factual data. The project activities consisted of a pilot workshop followed by a finalisation workshop with appropriate background analysis wrapped around each key event. The workshops involved the regional sales and marketing directors, a particularly independent set of wild cats. My role here as strategy leader was a cross between wild dog and hyena – responsible for directing the project, but also, as global marketing director, 'the man from head office there to help'. The lion here was a very charismatic CEO whose strong sponsorship helped to get people's attention.

Having won agreement from the team regarding the format and having set the workshop dates, the unanimous cry was "we can't do this until we have enough hard data". The general consensus was that we needed to commission fresh market research in each region and have some consultants develop models for market development backed up by significant channel restructuring and promotions. Not only was there insufficient time for such studies, but arguably, this level of data analysis was actually contrary to the essential aim of the strategic initiative. This was more about sharing a diverse set of good practice than about finding answers by number-crunching. This therefore relied more on tapping the collective wisdom and judgement of the team, and less on extensive analysis of external data. To enable this cross-fertilisation process, we decided to collate a set of comparative data covering each region that would help to highlight the key areas of outstanding performance for sharing with the group. These were carefully defined as:

- Volumes sold by product for each region
- Average profitability by product across all regions
- Packaging costs by high running product for each region
- Outline competitive analysis by region.

The pilot workshop was then structured as a creative brainstorming activity followed by evaluation aiming to find the key opportunities for synergy. The data was used as a fact-based resource to help guide the creative process. The result was to develop four pragmatic themes of value creation:

- Gap filling i.e. launching successful products from certain regions into new regions
- Co-ordinated growth campaign on high margin products (with shared promotion costs)
- Harmonised packaging design on certain high runners (to reduce costs)
- Co-ordinated approach between regions on shared key accounts.

Between the pilot and finalisation workshops, each region was required to carry out detailed analysis to confirm the potential across the four strategic themes within their region, and to develop implementation plans and resource needs. The result was a robust plan which delivered $15m of additional annual profits (5% profit growth for the group) in just one year. It had taken six weeks to develop and agree this strategy across a diverse business. It required the herding of some particularly independently minded wild cats. Relevant hard data and directed analysis were used to inform the strategy, but mainly to support the creativity of the people that knew the business, who utilised a great deal of wisdom and gut-feel to find the critical drivers of value.

TOP TIP
Prepare a package of useful factual data and distribute this in advance of major workshop activities for participants to pre-read and then use as a resource.

Rule 11 – FIND THE RIGHT LEVEL OF DATA

Data collection and analysis are crucial to defining a robust strategy but this can also be time-consuming. It is important to keep a balanced perspective, and to make sure that all data analysis is relevant and useful.

	Practical Tips – Getting the Right Level of Data
23	**Second guess the answer to help with data collection** It never does any harm to guess the likely outcome of the project early on. While this is bound to change as you go, it is a useful framework for understanding what data will be needed.
24	**Bundle up data needs and make the minimum individual requests** Inevitably you will need to ask marketing or finance people for the data you need which will add to their workload. There is nothing worse than receiving an endless number of piecemeal requests for slightly different variations of the same data. Take great care in thinking through exactly what data you need before tapping into the limited goodwill of the internal suppliers.
25	**Make sure there is a clear purpose for all data collected** It is often tempting to present as much data as possible to a project team just in case it proves relevant. Try to limit data to that which you are confident will be needed. Otherwise, people will get buried in detail and lose sight of the objectives.
26	**Data analysis should support strategic thinking, not lead it** Many strategy projects jump into detailed data analysis (e.g. discounted cash-flows, computer optimisation) too early in the process. Innovative strategic concepts are best developed by creative and insightful dialogue between knowledgeable managers supported with relevant facts. Data-crunching can then be used to test, fine tune and confirm the thinking.
27	**Respect both the data-junkies and the data-phobes** There seem to be two broad categories of strategy project participants. Data-junkies are those that can't even consider forward planning until they are comfortably surrounded by relevant data. Data-phobes are those that only want to deal with high-level concepts and ideas (leaving the data work to others). Make sure that the data-junkies have a regular fix of data to hand, but avoid inflicting allergic reaction on the data-phobes.

Rule 12 – ESTIMATE THE SIZE-OF-THE-PRIZE

The 'burning platform' was described earlier as the means of generating a sense of urgency at project launch. After the initial pilot and analysis work is complete, it is important to confirm the 'size-of-the-prize'. This is an early estimate of the likely benefits of the strategy – a crucial sanity check that helps to drive and focus the ongoing work.

Estimating the size-of-the-prize helps to focus and motivate the team

How to formulate the size-of-the-prize

The size-of-the-prize goes that one critical step further than doing a quick calculation on the back of an envelope. It needs to be based on an emerging rationale of the major strategic thrusts involving some approximate but well-judged analysis. This is usually possible during the pilot workshop and exploratory analysis phase. The aim here is to second-guess what the outcome of the strategy might look like, to paint an early vision of what the end state could be, in order to give the project a tangible destination and to confirm its vital importance. This helps to win ongoing support from senior stakeholders, provides a framework for focusing the ongoing project efforts, and serves to re-energise the team for the next stages of the journey.

CASE STUDY – **Global Production Strategy**

THE SIZE-OF-THE-PRIZE

The first stages of the strategy development work indicate that:
- Consolidating some of our primary production into fewer sites will provide significant benefits in terms of utilisation of capital intensive processes.
- Moving some of our labour-intensive finishing processes to low-labour-cost countries will support significant product cost savings.
- Coupling the above with an enhanced modular design concept will enable a late customisation model. This, in turn, will enable tailored products at faster lead-times with inherently low costs.
- Introducing specialist agile plants in major markets for customised, make-to-order products will serve premium-margin market segments.

Specific benefits targeted include:
- Reduced total global costs of 20%.
- Customer lead-time on mainstream products reduced from 5 to 2 days.
- Growth of 30% pa in premium-margin, make-to-order business.

CASE STUDY – **Business Process Re-engineering Strategy**

THE SIZE-OF-THE-PRIZE

The initial scoping of this project indicates that:
- Re-engineering our business processes around the latest business systems software will bring major benefits in terms of productivity, quality and customer responsiveness.
- Co-ordinating this across our global business will constitute a major advantage over the local, low-cost competitors who are a growing threat.

Specific benefits targeted include:
- Reducing lead-time on delivery of products from 12 to 8 weeks through better project execution.
- Increased production productivity by 15% (resulting in fewer temporary employees and less unplanned overtime).
- Reduced contract overruns and warranty claims by 25% (achieved via improved contract execution and risk management procedures in bidding, design office, production and installation).

Rule 13 – EXPLOIT THE ORGANISATIONAL DYNAMICS

There is a strong case for understanding and aligning the broader organisational dynamics with the project objectives and structure. One primary consideration is to understand the project's unique customer–supplier relationships. Another aspect is aligning the dynamics of the matrix structure to the strategy as it emerges. This sometimes means changing the organisation to fit the project!

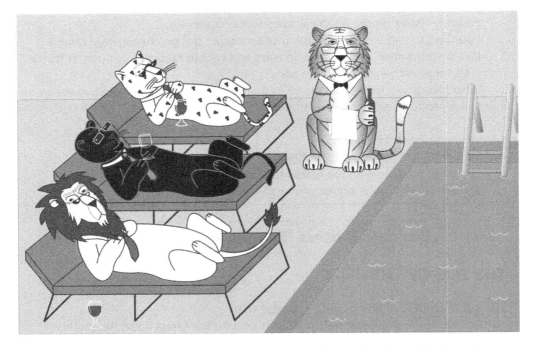

It is important to understand the unique customer–supplier relationships within the project

Why it's important to understand the customer–supplier relationship

The advantage of understanding the project's customer–supplier relationship is that it helps to clarify respective roles of different contributors at different points in the project life-cycle. For example, the emphasis in the early stages is generally for the internal customers to specify what they need. The emphasis then naturally switches so that the internal suppliers are positioned centre-stage to explain how they will meet the needs. The project customer–supplier relationships are typically unique to the context and objectives of the project, and can be the same as, or different from, the natural relationships.

Examples of Different Project Customer–Supplier Relationships	
Global Production Strategy	For the *Global Production Strategy* case study, the global business units were the internal customers of the project, and the regional operations directors were the internal suppliers. In other words, the emphasis was on operations to deliver a step change in how it served the market-facing business units. In this case, the project dynamic was in-line with the usual business dynamic where production would be considered to be serving the 'front end' functions.
Business Process Re-engineering Strategy	For the *BPR Strategy* case study, the dynamic was different. Here all the main business functions were internal customers of the project, with the management information services function acting as the internal supplier (responsible for business systems and business processes).
Global Marketing Strategy	For the *Global Marketing Strategy* case study, the project relationship was completely reversed from the normal dynamic. This involved all the global marketing directors identifying synergies across a diverse multi-national group. Here the marketing functions were internal suppliers to the project with the operational and all other functions acting as the internal customers receiving suggestions for value-adding initiatives.

Why change the organisation to fit the project?

Organisational redesign is a common means of implementing strategy so it is only natural that it is often sensible to alter the organisation as the strategy starts to emerge. A good example from the *Global Production Strategy* project involved the adjustment of the 'fixed' and 'dotted' line responsibilities in the overall matrix structure. The fixed lines i.e. those defining the major lines of business accountability, changed during the project from a regional axis to a global axis. This redistributed the main power within the organisation to the global product line businesses and away from the regional businesses. This change was implemented to ensure that a globally optimised strategy took emphasis over local considerations. It should be noted that, several years later, the 'fixed lines' reverted to regional accountability to drive better customer focus (demonstrating that organisational design often changes to fit the strategic needs of the day).

Rule 14 – EXPOSE THE BREAKTHROUGH POINT

Strategy development can tend to polarise around two extremes – constraint-driven improvements on today or sexy blue sky thinking on what might be possible. The former can lack ambition and the latter is often not realistic. Both of these are useful calibration points, but the best answer lies somewhere between. Breakthrough strategy refers to that elusive middle ground – the point that represents new, visionary thinking that is also practical and doable. Getting to breakthrough requires a particular approach, constant iteration and dogged determination.

It is important to get the right balance between ambition and achievability

Defining the spectrum of possibility

The first trick in finding the breakthrough point is to understand the extremes of the spectrum of possibility. The left hand end represents incremental thinking i.e. fixing known problems or tackling known opportunities. The right hand represents 'blue sky' or 'clean sheet' thinking. This completely ignores today and considers radical changes – things that we might want to do if we had the chance to start from scratch with limitless capital availability. Both ways of thinking are meaningful inputs as they define the boundaries, but neither represents the point where benefits significantly outweigh costs.

Finding the breakthrough point

The 'structured journey of discovery' approach to strategy is designed to gradually build the high level of intensity required to reveal the breakthrough point. The 'burning platform' has provided a sense of urgency during the early stages of the project. The pilot and exploratory stages have introduced new ways of thinking and new principles for future operation culminating in an assessment of the 'size-of-the-prize'. The aggregation activity has allowed the new ideas to mature and synthesise into a compelling new story. Ongoing analysis is revealing a deep understanding of the key drivers and mechanisms for creating strategic value. The cumulative effect has been to gradually build a heightened awareness of the critical issues and the most exciting opportunities.

At the same time, political tensions have increased as the possible future world has started to become clear. The prospect of real change has upset the delicate equilibrium within the jungle and some wild cats are feeling threatened.

The point of maximum tension occurs during the finalisation activity and this requires careful facilitation by the strategy leader. This event is usually a 2– or 3–day activity (including, importantly, the evenings in between). The project team often feels excitement, anxiety and frustration in equal measures. The finalisation activity starts to solve outstanding issues in some areas but also sparks off confusion and mini-feuds in others.

Suddenly a paradigm shift occurs as a natural consequence of the accumulated tension. More often than not, this occurs overnight aided by informal discussion over dinner and in the bar. This is usually the combination of a breakthrough in thinking coupled with a breakthrough in political harmony all rolled into one. The breakthrough point is now clear to all.

Finding the breakthrough point therefore requires consistent and prolonged effort at every point on this guided journey. This culminates in deeper levels of understanding and heightened levels of tension all at the same time. At that point, with careful stewardship from the strategy leader, a little piece of magic occurs!

TOP TIP

Make sure you sit next to the senior stakeholders and opinion-leaders at the dinners between workshop days. This is where breakthroughs are primed.

Rule 15 – DEFINE HOW TO MAKE IT HAPPEN

Strategy is clearly no use to anyone without implementation, and, as the new way of thinking starts to emerge, we need to start working out what we are actually going to do. It is useful to think of implementation projects in two categories. 'Foundation projects' are the major early strategic thrusts that will develop clear momentum and deliver quick wins. 'Enabling projects' often sit more in the background but are just as important in ensuring the success of the overall programme.

CASE STUDY – **Business Process Re-engineering Strategy**

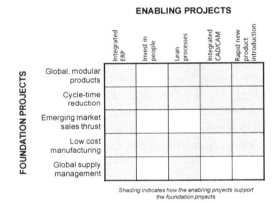

Shading indicates how the enabling projects support the foundation projects

The *BPR Strategy* project was about a lot more than just new systems and processes. It needed to demonstrate radical changes in the business and tangible benefits. The distinction between foundation projects and enabling projects was useful here (with the former geared more at real business improvements and the latter aimed at the systems and processes). The chart opposite shows the outcome as a matrix showing how the various enabling projects supported the key foundation projects. One other key aspect was that the foundation projects were led by the main operational managers (in sales, production, procurement etc) with the enabling projects led by the supporting functions (management information systems, human resources etc).

CASE STUDY – **Global Production Strategy**

The *Global Production Strategy* project culminated in a similar distinction between foundation and enabling projects. The foundation projects involved tangible reconfiguration of the global production footprint led by the regional operations directors. The enabling projects covered internal and external communications, finance and legal aspects led by the head office support functions.

Rule 16 – MOVE FROM PLANNING TO DOING

A common problem in traditional approaches to strategy development is that, even when the final strategy has been agreed, there is huge inertia that delays the launch of implementation. There are various ways of ensuring that the transition from 'planning' to 'doing' is seamless.

	Practical Tips – Ensuring Seamless Transition to Implementation
28	**Seed implementation champions into the strategy process** Ideally the champions who will drive implementation should be part of the core strategy team from the outset (or at the very least during the finalisation stages). Hand-over of accountability from the 'planners' to the 'doers' is the classic cause of loss of momentum.
29	**Dedicate 50% of the finalisation workshop to implementation planning** Implementation planning is not a background activity – it needs the combined experience and judgement of the team to ensure do-ability.
30	**Identify clear accountability for each implementation project** The finalisation event also serves to clarify who-does-what, and who is responsible.
31	**Develop a sense of competition between implementation champions** Having the implementation champions formulating their plans together with their peers naturally generates a constructively competitive dynamic.
32	**Identify tangible incentives for delivery** These should be at individual as well as team levels, and linked to the project measures of success.
33	**Don't demobilise until the quick wins are secured** The great temptation when the strategy is agreed is to breathe a sigh of relief and hand over to the implementation team. The ideal time to demobilise the team is 3–6 months further on, after a formal audit event, where tangible progress is evident and teething problems have been solved.

TOP TIP

As strategy leader, insist that your role does not end until at least the first major implementation milestone is successfully reached.

C
FOUR MODEL WORKSHOP FORMATS

Overview
Pilot Workshop
Aggregation Workshop
Finalisation Workshop
Audit Workshop

OVERVIEW

Workshops are fundamental to the development of strategy in the modern, flat, empowered organisation. They are the basis for creating breakthrough thinking and for building ownership and accountability. It is the strategy leader's responsibility to successfully orchestrate these vital activities. This section presents a range of model workshop formats to fit with every stage of the strategy development life-cycle.

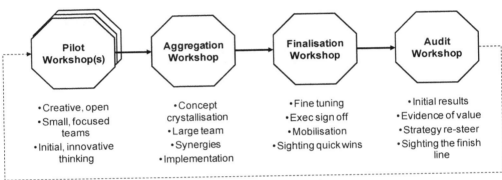

Strategy development life-cycle

Four types of strategy workshop

The chart above shows four different types of workshop that fit with the various stages of the strategy development life-cycle. The nature of each workshop type is very different in terms of scope, maturity of data, the balance of creativity and evaluation, and the numbers of people involved. Each workshop type requires a fundamentally different approach in designing the format, detailed activities and facilitation plans. Each type is outlined opposite, and described more fully in the following pages, illustrated using the real-life strategy success stories.

Description	Inputs	Outputs
Pilot workshop Multiple pilot workshops help break the project into small chunks. This is the most creative part of the process and each pilot requires relatively small teams of clear thinkers. This generates a good dynamic for engaging in brainstorming activities and for developing the basic strategic concepts.	Contextual data Ideas	Concepts Working propositions
Aggregation workshop This is the vehicle for combining outputs from the various pilot workshops and any subsequent exploratory analysis. This major event often marks a key transition from creativity to practicality, and helps to crystallise, harmonise and simplify the underpinning strategic concepts. The aggregation workshop is more complex to facilitate. It has multiple inputs and needs to involve a larger group of representatives. The result is a confirmed strategic logic, agreed measures and targets, a clear future vision, and the outline plan for how to get there.	Pilot workshop outputs Exploratory analysis	Integrated concepts Ideal future state Outline transition plan
Finalisation workshop This is crunch time. Confirming analysis has been carried out including investment cases and support plans for the HR, legal and communications functions. The full executive board is involved plus the implementation team. This is an opportunity for final fine tuning, and for focusing on what is required to mobilise the strategy and secure quick wins.	Confirming analysis Draft final strategy	Confirmed strategy & implementation plan
Audit workshop This is timed early on during implementation and is a formal opportunity to understand any early lessons. Focus is on driving through the quick wins that secure momentum. Any necessary re-steering of the strategy is considered. Sights are set on the finish line to help recharge the team.	Teething problems Early successes Project scorecard	Corrective actions Strategy tune-up

PILOT WORKSHOP

The pilot workshop is the most creative element of the strategy development process and the format, participants, style and environment need to reflect this. The basic flow of activities typically follows a divergent then convergent process. This ensures that we cover the full spectrum of possibility but then focus on what is truly value-adding and practical.

Format

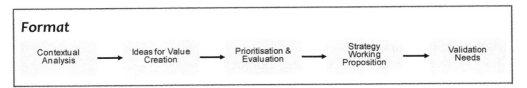

Contextual Analysis → Ideas for Value Creation → Prioritisation & Evaluation → Strategy Working Proposition → Validation Needs

Inputs
Contextual data
Ideas

Outputs
Strategic concepts
Strategy working proposition

Duration
1–2 days

No. of participants
6–16 (more if the group Is split)

Type of participants
Subject experts
External advisers
Mix of chiefs and indians

Key dynamic
Creative and expansive

Description

Pilot workshops are the foundation of creative strategies. They need to be fresh, dynamic and inspiring. They should also create outputs that are meaningful and practical. Hence they should follow a divergent then convergent process, first allowing expansive thought and then filtering the outputs to make them fit reality.

The raw materials for pilots are people with ideas (plus a limited amount of contextual data). The people who run the business all have their pet theories on strategic development. These need extracting and channelling to provide a 'working proposition' for a strategy. This is about getting everyone on the same page regarding the key drivers, trends and creative opportunities. There is clearly a need for validating analysis, but this can be done after the essential strategic concepts have been clarified.

The politics of pilot workshops are relatively benign as the general mood is open and positive. However, some participants may already be predicting the outcome and jostling for position.

Typical Pilot Workshop Activities	
Contextual Analysis	o Review of external data and pre-prepared digests o Charting of key trends (using, for example, SWOT or roadmapping techniques) o Getting everyone to a common level of understanding
Ideas for Value Creation	o Creative brainstorming on possible areas of value creation o Multi-dimensional to cover all aspects / for out-of-box thinking o Often involves external stimulus to counter parochialism o Cross-functional peer review to expand horizons
Prioritisation & Evaluation	o First-stage prioritisation (often involving voting-type method e.g. sticky dots) o Clustering of ideas into meaningful strategic concepts o Expansion and evaluation of key strategic concepts o Assessment based on quantitative and qualitative success factors
Strategy Working Proposition	o Creation of possible future scenarios based on concepts so far o First-pass definition of preferred future scenario (e.g. 5–year vision) o First-pass definition of implementation steps required to deliver the vision o Estimation of the possible size-of-the-prize
Validation Needs	o Identification of analysis requirements to explore and validate the proposition o Clarification of who-does-what o Identification of any communication needs to other pilot activities o Confirmation of next milestone activity e.g. aggregation workshop

Typical workshop techniques used in pilot workshops (roughly in the sequence in which they might be used)	
Formal brainstorm – see page 70	Clustering – see page 102
Break-out brainstorm – see page 73	Weighted criteria scoring – see page 110
Dot prioritisation – see page 98	Carousel brainstorm – see page 77

CASE STUDY – **BPR Strategy Pilot Workshop**

	DAY 1	DAY 2
MORNING	BRIEF	
	SWOT	WORKSTREAM DEFINITION BY SUB-GROUP
	IDEAS FOR VALUE CREATION	
AFTERNOON	PRIORITISATION	GROUP CHALLENGE & IMPROVE
	CLUSTERING	WORKSTREAM MOBILISATION
	WORKSTREAM CREATION	WRAP UP & NEXT STEPS

The *BPR Strategy* project made extensive use of pilot workshops. To recap, this project was aiming to improve operational performance across all business functions in a large global organisation. The backdrop was the introduction of new business systems software and hardware but, in some respects, this was a secondary issue. The really exciting underlying opportunity was to make a step change in the way the company did business. This project was also an important exercise in empowerment with key staff at all levels involved in deciding and then implementing the strategy.

The project format, as previously described, involved multiple pilot workshops organised by business function (with an additional pilot workshop to define key interfaces between functions). The two-day workshop format is illustrated above and followed the typical pattern of divergent, creative thinking followed by convergent evaluation.

Each pilot workshop involved around 15 key staff from the respective function covering the various product lines and geographic regions providing a wonderfully diverse and vibrant resource – multi-cultural, varying backgrounds, different ages – all with common problems and a common desire to make things better. This was a project where herding the cats was relatively easy due to the naturally balanced team profiles and the pre-dominance of potential winners over potential losers.

The output from each pilot was a working proposition strategy for that function detailing the high priority strategic thrusts required to improve operational effectiveness. This was supported by an ongoing plan to further analyse and validate the strategy. The by-product of each workshop was an energised and aligned set of champions for helping to make this happen.

Practical Tips – Leading Pilot Workshops

34 | **More doing than listening**
A pilot workshop is a creative activity. Listening to briefs or presentations should be limited. A good rule of thumb is 80/20 doing/listening.

35 | **More wall-charts than PowerPoint**
Try to have the workshop deliverables visible to all participants at all times. This helps cross-fertilisation of ideas. Wall-charts work best for this. (Obviously with PowerPoint only one slide can be seen at once).

36 | **Cover the walls with an emerging story**
A growing set of wall-charts builds an unfolding story of the strategy coming together.

37 | **Get the team to spend time on its feet**
Don't spend a whole workshop sitting down. Get people on their feet writing on charts or presenting feedback. It's amazing how physical mobility aids mental mobility.

38 | **Be wary of the 'So what?' question**
Sometimes the relevance of a particular activity may not be absolutely clear, resulting in the dreaded 'So what?' question. Always be ready to explain how the outputs are building towards a result aligned with the objectives.

39 | **Know the difference between 'exhaustive' and 'exhausting'**
Creating a diverse range of ideas often means long brainstorming sessions. Don't let it go on so long that people get tired or bored. When the quality of the outputs starts to tail off, re-focus and re-energise or move on.

40 | **Everyone must contribute, no-one should dominate**
In good workshops everyone needs to get involved. Some naturally take the lead or are more engaged than others. Don't let leading turn into domination. Gently invite naturally quiet people to share their views and thoughts.

41 | **Summarise after every major activity**
Workshops are intense and draining – someone at every point will be losing the plot. Use each scheduled break to summarise what we've done, and where we're going.

42 | **Manage moments of tension and release**
Tension is a natural part of the creative process. People's brains are over-flowing and comfort zones are being tested. Predict (or even plan) the points of tension, and provide a mechanism for release.

43 | **Use little bits of humour, fun and drama**
These spice things up and keep everyone engaged. But be careful poking fun at anyone in particular. Even the most seasoned wild cats can be sensitive and public humiliation strikes deep.

AGGREGATION WORKSHOP

Aggregation workshops are used to merge the outputs from multiple pilot studies. This, by definition, involves a large group of wild cats and a large amount of input data. The ideal outcomes of aggregation are a harmonised strategy and extensive buy-in. Strong leadership and advanced techniques are needed to facilitate this high-stakes activity.

Format

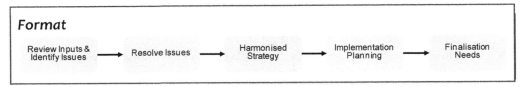

| Review Inputs & Identify Issues | → | Resolve Issues | → | Harmonised Strategy | → | Implementation Planning | → | Finalisation Needs |

Inputs
Working proposition strategies
Exploratory analysis

Outputs
Harmonised strategic concepts
Ideal future state
Outline transition plan

Duration
2–3 days

No. of participants
12–30

Type of participants
Pilot representatives
Executive board representatives
Implementation champions

Key dynamic
Practicality and challenge

Description

This is a major milestone in the strategy 'journey of discovery' where the dynamic shifts from creativity and exploration to challenge and practicality. The first activity is to review the pilot inputs and identify issues, gaps and inconsistencies. These are then resolved (usually by break-out groups) before a harmonised strategy is constructed. This typically takes the form of an agreed future vision and a set of underpinning strategic concepts. This describes the future business in a completely different way.

In addition, the aggregation workshop should start to build an outline implementation plan. The act of thinking through how to achieve the desired future state exerts a further 'pressure test' on the practicality of the emerging strategy, and drives ongoing refinement. This should be led by the implementation champions to start to build accountability.

The stakes are high during aggregation as the prospect of disrupting comfort zones becomes more real. This requires firm and creative leadership and specific facilitation techniques.

Typical Aggregation Workshop Activities	
Review Inputs & Identify Issues	o Review of pilot study recommendations o Identification of issues, gaps and inconsistencies o Prioritisation and clustering of issues
Resolve Issues	o Break-out group activity by issue cluster o Resolution of issues and filling of gaps where possible o Suggested harmonisation of inconsistencies within pilot recommendations o Peer review of outcome and refinements
Harmonised Strategy	o Review of future options (at aggregated, enterprise level) o Option evaluation and definition of ideal future state (at enterprise level) o Definition of success factors and targets o Confirmation of the size-of-the-prize (at enterprise level)
Implementation Planning	o Identification of foundation projects required for implementation o First-pass definition of implementation plans by project o First-pass definition of business case by project o Peer review of outcome and refinement
Finalisation Needs	o Identification of analysis requirements to finalise the strategy o Identification of enabling projects (that cut across foundation projects) o Clarification of who-does-what regarding finalisation o Confirmation of next milestone activity e.g. finalisation workshop

Typical workshop techniques used in aggregation workshops (roughly in the sequence in which they might be used)	
Gallery walk & issue capture – see page 106	Weighted criteria scoring – see page 110
Dot prioritisation – see page 98	Storyboarding – see page 86
Clustering – see page 102	Bubble charts – see page 114
Option / scenario development – see page 81	Carousel brainstorm – see page 77

CASE STUDY – **Global Production Strategy**

	DAY 1	DAY 2
MORNING	BRIEF	REGIONAL AGGREGATION & SYNERGIES
	PRODUCT LINE STRATEGIES – Review & issue identification	
AFTERNOON	PRODUCT LINE STRATEGIES – Resolve issues & harmonise	REGIONAL IMPLEMENTATION PLANS
	PERFORMANCE MEASURES & TARGETS	FINALISATION STEPS

As described earlier, this project involved identical pilot workshops across four global product lines, followed by an aggregation workshop to merge the four pilot recommendations. Here the global product line heads were positioned as 'internal customers' who were defining their needs in terms of production performance. The regional operations heads (for three regions – Americas, Europe and Asia) were positioned as the 'internal suppliers' who were tasked with delivering the strategy. This key event involved 2 senior representatives from each product line and each region, plus 2 functional representatives from technology, finance, HR and marketing, plus the core project team of 4 – all adding up to a heady mix of 26 wild cats!

The first day of the workshop involved intense review and harmonisation of the global product line strategies. This required strong and creative intervention by myself as strategy leader to negotiate resolutions to critical issues. One example of this was to broker agreement to a completely new framework for defining the different roles of plants within the global network. This was essential to future restructuring and needed a number of paradigm shifts away from old ways of thinking.

The second day saw a shift from global product line focus to regional operations focus. This aligned with a shift towards implementation planning, with the regional operations heads taking accountability. The shift to regional focus also enabled the definition of significant synergies by optimising the implementation approach across the product lines.

The outcome of the workshop was a harmonised strategy and an outline plan for implementation, all agreed and owned by a wide range of stakeholders. An exciting strategy was beginning to form but this still required a great deal of financial evaluation and refinement before it could be finalised.

Practical Tips – Leading Aggregation Workshops

44 ### Meet the evening before for the briefing
With large groups typically converging from far-flung places, it makes sense to have a formal evening event the day before. This enables everyone to re-engage with the project and catch up with each other.

45 ### Pre-define break-out teams where possible
In most circumstances, having at least a draft plan helps to ensure seamless transitions between plenary and sub-group activities. Last-minute adjustments can obviously be allowed if needed.

46 ### Be careful to balance break-out teams
The general rules are that break-out teams should be led by the problem owner, and involve a cross-functional mix (or cross-regional where relevant). Take care to avoid any longstanding character clashes.

47 ### Look for opportunities to harmonise
Harmonising strategic concepts developed by separate teams is a critical aggregation activity. The workshop process will naturally drive harmonisation, but also actively intervene to ensure inconsistencies are resolved.

48 ### Develop a new, common language via harmonisation
Innovative strategies usually create a new language for the organisation. This embodies the necessary paradigm shifts. Actively suggest and test new terms with clear definitions so that everybody knows what these mean.

49 ### Simple is much harder than complex
This really comes to life in aggregation workshops when there is a mass of conceptual thinking to digest. Plan time for simplification and clarification. Use evening work where possible to reflect then play back suggestions next day.

50 ### Arrange an external speaker
Having a relevant guest speaker (perhaps from a different company which has been through a similar strategic transition) is an ideal activity for freshening the thinking part-way through an intense aggregation workshop.

51 ### Instil an increasing sense of urgency
Aggregation events are intense and need a strong sense of urgency to succeed. 'This is a one-time opportunity to transform the business.' 'The investment in time so far is significant.' 'This team needs to show a result.'

52 ### Expect ongoing refinements and iteration
Don't expect strategy workshops to directly deliver finished, detailed strategies. Workshops are great for developing innovative concepts and for merging data and experience. Finalised strategies require significant ongoing analysis and iteration.

FINALISATION WORKSHOP

The finalisation workshop is the last chance to refine the strategy before significant investment is committed, communications launched, and reputations put on the line. Suddenly the prospect of significant disruption to the business is very real. Key risks need to be assessed and implementation plans adjusted to ensure early success.

Format

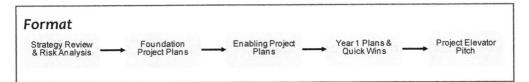

| Strategy Review & Risk Analysis | → | Foundation Project Plans | → | Enabling Project Plans | → | Year 1 Plans & Quick Wins | → | Project Elevator Pitch |

Inputs
Final draft strategy
Financial analysis

Outputs
Confirmed strategy
Foundation project plans
Enabling project plans

Duration
2–3 days

No of participants
12–30

Type of participants
Pilot representatives
Full executive board
Implementation champions

Key dynamic
Fine-tuning
Energising launch

Description

The draft strategy is now mature and based on harmonised, innovative concepts. But this is much more than just a sign-off exercise. The risks associated with breakthrough change are, by definition, very high and this is the last chance to have all the major players in one room for an extended period. This is a key opportunity to iron out any remaining wrinkles, and to 'pressure test' the implementation plans. This requires all the senior wild cats to take one last hard look before pushing the button.

Risk analysis and fine-tuning are core activities within this final event. In addition, detailed plans for foundation projects and enabling projects need to be developed and agreed. These could cover major change five or ten years into the future. However, the Year 1 plan is most important. The strategy will need to deliver visible progress and hard benefits within months if it is going to survive its infancy. The Year 1 plans, targets, and accountabilities are critical outputs.

The last task is to step back and define the essence of the strategy to form an elevator pitch as a final check on integrity.

Typical Finalisation Workshop Activities	
Strategy Review & Risk Analysis	o Review of final draft strategy recommendations o Identification of key risks and uncertainties o Prioritisation and clustering of risks and uncertainties
Foundation Project Plans	o Break-out group activity by foundation project o Resolution of key risks and uncertainties where possible o Finalisation of foundation project plans, accountabilities and resources o Peer review of outcome and refinements
Enabling Project Plans	o Break-out group activity by enabling project o Resolution of key risks and uncertainties where possible o Finalisation of enabling project plans, accountabilities and resources o Peer review of outcome and refinements
Year 1 Plans & Quick Wins	o Break-out group activity by foundation and enabling project o Detailed action planning over initial 12 months o Clarification of milestones and quantified business benefits o Peer review of outcome and refinement
Project Elevator Pitch	o Identification of 'strategy essence' as an elevator pitch o Translation into core messages for project communications covering customers, employees, shareholders etc

Typical workshop techniques used in finalisation workshops (roughly in the sequence in which they might be used)	
Gallery walk & issue capture – see page 106	Storyboarding – see page 86
Traffic light analysis – see page 119	Action planning – see page 91
Dot prioritisation – see page 98	Break-out brainstorm – see page 73
Clustering – see page 102	

CASE STUDY – **Global Production Strategy**

DAY 1	DAY 2
MORNING BRIEF	ENABLING PROJECT PLANNING
FINE POLISHING & RISK ANALYSIS	
AFTERNOON FOUNDATION PROJECT PLANNING	YEAR 1 PLANS & QUICK WINS
	ELEVATOR PITCH

It was now clear that this was a major transformation project for the company that would involve significant restructuring of the production footprint. The investment would require external finance so the initiative would form the major part of the approaching annual results presentation to shareholders. There were 36 participants in the finalisation workshop including the full executive board, senior managers from product line and regional operations, and corporate functional heads including HR, legal, communications and finance functions. The finalisation workshop was held in an off-site location with the format illustrated. The atmosphere was one of excitement and anxiety in equal measures.

The first day was designed to deal with the anxieties while reinforcing the excitement. The inputs included summary strategies for global product lines and regional operations which reflected a huge amount of work carried out to date. The gallery walk technique (see p 106) was used to review these inputs using a simple risk analysis framework. The risks were assessed and prioritised, and allocated to the relevant foundation and enabling projects accordingly.

Break-out groups were then run for detailing the project plans including risk mitigation measures. This covered foundation projects first, and enabling projects second, with carefully designed teams used to promote cross-alignment and accountability. These were followed by a more detailed Year 1 planning session which crucially identified the tangible results expected over the first 12 months. The workshop concluded with a facilitated session to crystallise the 'elevator pitch' for the project.

The result of the finalisation workshop was to effectively mobilise the entire management team for radical change. The formal public launch of the project followed shortly afterwards and the foundation projects drove real changes within weeks.

53

Create simple, standard templates for all inputs

There is now a great deal of data to deal with so having consistent, easily digestible overviews is essential to support common understanding of all the prior efforts.

54

Have all the detail to hand as a back-up in an accessible form

Not all the detailed work will be needed but, when it is, there will be an urgent need to access it. The right details must then be ready and directly useable.

55

Don't get lost in details

Tapping into the well of detail may cause an uncontrollable spurt that washes everything away. Be clear on the reasons for tapping into detail and make sure the plug is reinserted as soon as you have tapped enough.

56

Invest in individual pre-briefings

Pre-discussions with each stakeholder are useful since at this late stage there is little room for error. The pre-briefing will often point to key technical or political barriers that can be addressed before or during the workshop.

57

Promote constructive tension and internal competition

Workshops thrive on constructive tension and this is to be encouraged as long as there are clear mechanisms to release the tension. Internal competition between key contributors and champions can also be a healthy dynamic.

58

Call special 'issue resolution' break-outs where required

When tensions get too high, pull a small group of senior stakeholders into a quiet room to bash out a solution. The rest of the workshop can continue as planned, and this team can report back when they have a proposal. This is often successful in resolving any protracted political feuds or entrenched positions.

59

Arrange a real customer to speak at the middle evening

One great way of reminding everyone what this is all about is to have a (friendly, longstanding) customer give a dinner speech on the middle evening (pitched around how the project will support his/her future requirements).

60

Cross-check financials for consistency

Each pilot team will have developed financial models for the various projects and, despite common guidelines, these will inevitably still vary in certain details. Finalisation is the last opportunity to drive out anomalies and ensure consistency.

61

Reinforce the short-term plan as well as the distant vision

Most strategists thrive on painting an inspiring future vision long into the distance. This is undoubtedly valuable but, at the finalisation stage, we also need to help everyone visualise what this means in one year and two years from now. This gives the project a feeling of immediacy and substance. It also ensures that the key players commit to targets that they will have to deliver before their next career change!

AUDIT WORKSHOP

The audit workshop is the ideal hand-over point from strategy leader to implementation leader. This is because strategy is an inexact science, an aim/ fire/re-aim process, and learning from early experiences is crucial. The ideal timing is a few months in – far enough for the initial chaos to subside but early enough for corrective actions to be arranged.

Format

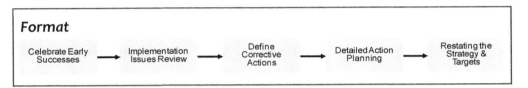

Inputs
Teething problems
Early successes
Project scorecard results

Outputs
Corrective actions
Updated strategy
Revised targets

Duration
1–2 days

No of participants
12–20

Type of participants
Implementation champions
Functional representatives
Steering group

Key dynamic
Trouble-shooting problems
Celebrating early successes

Description

This is a formal opportunity for standing back, taking stock of the experiences and lessons so far, and for creatively readjusting the direction. It works best with a relatively small group of implementation champions and key representatives from the project's internal customers and suppliers.

The positive way to start is to recognise and celebrate successes but this then becomes a predominantly trouble-shooting activity. Teething problems are reviewed and clustered and working groups deployed to define corrective actions. These then require detailing and planning with accountabilities agreed. This is also the first opportunity to review early results against the project scorecard. This should drive prioritisation of corrective action and inform a first review of the forecast targets.

The audit workshop should culminate in identifying areas where the strategy itself requires adjusting. This is now the point where the strategy leader can, with confidence, hand over.

Typical Audit Workshop Activities	
Celebrate Early Successes	○ Review of project scorecard results ○ Recognition of what has gone well so far
Implementation Issues Review	○ Review and refinement of pre-prepared issues lists ○ Prioritisation of key issues ○ Clustering of key issues ○ Identification of corrective action workstreams and responsibilities
Define Corrective Actions	○ Break-out group activity by workstream ○ Resolution of key issues or plans for resolution ○ Peer review of outcome and refinements
Detailed Action Planning	○ Break-out group activity to detail formal action plans ○ Clarification of resources and accountabilities ○ Peer review of outcome and refinement
Restating the Strategy & Targets	○ Review of strategy to identify necessary adjustments ○ Review and update of forecast project costs ○ Review and update of forecast project benefits

Typical workshop techniques used in audit workshops	
(roughly in the sequence in which they might be used)	
Gallery walk & issue capture – see page 106	Break-out brainstorm – see page 73
Dot prioritisation – see page 98	Storyboarding – see page 86
Clustering – see page 102	Action planning – see page 91

CASE STUDY – **BPR Strategy**

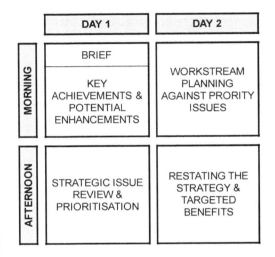

This project was launched via a big bang start-up of new business systems with an irreversible switch to completely new business practices. The first few weeks of running using the 'new way' were extremely chaotic and disruptive. A mix of operator error, software bugs, data transfer problems and a steep learning curve made for a complex, issue-resolution firestorm. This incurred significant extra costs and even impacted customer deliveries. The pressure to turn things around quickly was intense and, after 3 months of concerted effort, many of the major problems were patched up. For the first time, there was some breathing space. This was the ideal time to hold the audit workshop.

This two-day event involved a small, focused team of 12 participants including global representatives for each business function (sales, marketing, engineering, procurement, production, aftermarket, finance) assisted by the core project team and the systems experts. This team was weary from a long period of fire-fighting so it was important that the workshop stepped to a fresh and different level. This was achieved initially by focusing on the key achievements and understanding how to secure and enhance these. This was followed by a review of the strategic challenges that still required attention with prioritisation and clustering.

For the second day the team was split into sub-groups to tackle the high priority clusters of issues. This resulted in co-ordinated corrective actions covering amended business procedures, adjustments to ERP software, and retraining of key staff. These revised approaches were rolled out globally via the functional peer groups.

The final workshop activity involved restating the complete strategy and refining the targeted benefits in the context of the adjustments made after 3 months of operation. The overall outcome was a more robust plan for business transformation which was realised over the following years.

Practical Tips – Leading Audit Workshops

62 | ### Choose the right timing
This is a tricky balance – especially for the first audit. Too soon and everyone is still consumed by fire-fighting and not yet in the right mood for reflection. Too late and any required realignments will have been delayed and any negative impacts will have been extended (or even rendered irreversible). Within 3 to 6 months is ideal.

63 | ### Make sure the audit 'champions' are well prepared
These champions will typically be representing the interests of a cross-regional or cross-functional team so it is important that they have done their homework. One approach is to co-ordinate formal teleconference reviews around each champion's area of responsibility involving the full peer group to optimise the issues lists in advance of the formal workshop.

64 | ### Celebrate the progress-to-date and any early wins
Ideally there will be positives to draw out and it is important at the outset to re-motivate a team which will have been severely tested by the inevitable challenges of implementing major change. The majority of the audit is, by definition, problem-centred so this needs balancing or the team can get bogged down and negative.

65 | ### Prepare possible workstream titles in advance
The strategy leader will be able to view the combined issues lists before the workshop and should be able to 'best-guess' the emerging workstreams. This will help accelerate the critical point where the challenges are grouped and structured into sensible packages of ongoing work.

66 | ### Refine the workstream definitions again after Day 1
The strategy leader should be able to refine the workstream proposal again during the middle evening of a two-day event. It may also be helpful to test this with a smaller group of senior stakeholders over dinner.

67 | ### Smaller working groups sometimes require more coaching
In most of the break-out work described in the previous workshop formats, the sub-groups were larger and were facilitated by a natural senior 'owner' who was accountable for the ongoing activity. Here the sub-groups are smaller (perhaps 2 or 3) and the workstreams may be broader. There may be natural owners in the group but, even so, this requires more hands-on coaching of the groups. The strategy leader should rotate between the groups periodically to help develop high quality and consistent outputs.

D
SIX CREATIVE TECHNIQUES FOR WORKSHOPS

Overview
Formal Brainstorm
Break-out Brainstorm
Carousel Brainstorm
Option or Scenario Development
Storyboarding
Action Planning

OVERVIEW

One major benefit of strategy workshops is the opportunity for collective creativity involving some of the best brains in the business. But creative energies need directing and harnessing or group activity can soon descend into chaos. This section describes a selection of techniques for structuring creativity to get maximum value from this major investment in time, energy and money.

Workshops are great for creating bright ideas

Various creativity techniques

There are two main types of workshop activity: creativity and evaluation. This section deals with creativity, the next section with evaluation. Creativity has a number of typical forms when employed in workshops. Brainstorming is the archetypal workshop activity but strategy workshops often involve other forms including scenario development and 'storyboarding' (used here to describe a high-level project planning approach). Action planning is a further form (which tends to be one level down in detail as compared to storyboarding). These techniques are described in overview below and in more detail in the following subsections.

Technique	Description	Ideal use
Formal brainstorm	• Traditional, round-table brainstorming format • Participants contribute 1 idea each in strict rotation • Continue until ideas run dry	Small groups Breadth not depth Early on in pilots
Break-out brainstorm	• Involves splitting larger groups into teams • Each team considers a different perspective on the strategic challenge • Requires a template for guiding consistent inputs	Larger groups Depth and breadth Concept stages
Carousel brainstorm	• Involves splitting large groups into teams • Each team gets time at each of several stations to contribute ideas against a theme • Teams rotate to cover each station	Larger groups Energy boost Defining next steps
Option or scenario development	• Involves splitting large groups into teams • Each team focuses on developing a range of strategic options or future scenarios • Follows brainstorms and concept development • Requires a template for guiding consistent inputs	Range of options Depth and structure After concepts are clear
Storyboarding	• Used for high-level implementation planning • Captures actions on annual or quarterly basis • Includes other key elements of the 'story' e.g. costs, benefits, risks	For high-level visibility of possible implementation approach
Action planning	• Used for more detailed implementation planning • Usually follows storyboarding during the latter stages of the project • Captures tasks covering what, why, who, when	For detailed confirmation of more refined implementation plans

FORMAL BRAINSTORM

Most people are familiar with the classic 'formal brainstorm' where the team contributes one idea in turn and the process continues until the good ideas dry up. Quality of ideas can vary, however, and this technique is prone to becoming bogged down and mechanistic. This section describes a few tips for keeping this fresh, dynamic and high quality.

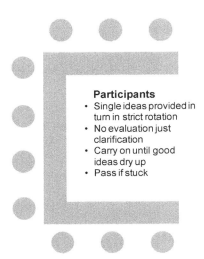

Ideal Application
- Groups of 6-12
- Breadth rather than depth
- Early in strategic process

Participants
- Single ideas provided in turn in strict rotation
- No evaluation just clarification
- Carry on until good ideas dry up
- Pass if stuck

Strategy Leader
- Clarifies the exact question being asked
- Captures ideas on post its or flip chart
- Clarifies meanings and assures quality
- Prevents repetition
- Keeps it fresh and lively
- Draws to a close when good ideas are drying up

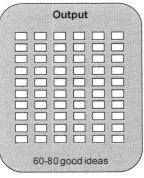

Output

60-80 good ideas

Duration
- 30-45 mins

Overview of technique

The formal brainstorm technique is illustrated above. This shows the participants arranged in a U-shape with the strategy leader orchestrating a structured process. The outputs are ideally displayed as created (often on post-its on a wall-chart).

How it works

The participants are asked to contribute ideas on a specific theme or question as defined by the strategy leader. Each participant provides one idea in strict rotation with the strategy leader capturing the ideas either directly on a flipchart or on individual post-its (which are immediately displayed on a wall-chart). Participants are not allowed to discuss, challenge or evaluate the ideas suggested (but they are allowed to request clarification). Participants can pass when they have run out of ideas. The strategy leader brings the brainstorm to a close when everyone has dried up. A typical output is 60–80 ideas covering a broad range.

Typical Duration

45 mins — A good time to allow for a formal brainstorm is 45 minutes. This should be enough time to generate a large number of ideas.

Advantages	Disadvantages
• This approach guarantees that everyone has an equal opportunity to make a contribution and nobody is allowed to dominate. • The output covers a wide range of possibilities in a short period of time. • Participants build on each other's ideas and this inspires greater creativity. • Everyone owns the outputs.	• Does not create any depth of idea development – more breadth than depth. • Can become mechanistic and sterile and needs careful facilitation. • Does not suit large groups (more than 10–12) as the wait for your turn becomes too long. • The exhaustive approach sometimes means that idea quality becomes diluted.

Ideal application

The formal brainstorm is the classic opening creative technique at the outset of a strategic process. It generally works best, therefore, early on in pilot workshops. It creates large quantities of ideas that can be quality controlled to a degree. It works best in relatively small groups (up to, say, 10 or 12 participants) but larger groups can be split into parallel sessions if required.

71

Practical Tips – Leading Formal Brainstorms

68 *Make sure the key question is crystal clear*
It is amazing how often participants try to answer a different question from the one set. Write the question very clearly on a flipchart. Read it out at the beginning and refer back to it if the any answers start to drift off-message.

69 *Ask for two minutes' private thought before kick-off*
This gets the participants to think before they speak. Suggest that they make a list. A few minutes' silence adds some dramatic tension to the proceedings and the kick-off is much more dynamic and positive.

70 *The outputs need to be visible to all participants at all times*
Visibility helps avoid repetition (and also helps to inspire inter-connected ideas or conceptual spin-offs). Post-its on wall-charts work best, but ideas written directly onto flipcharts also work (but this is not so easy to edit).

71 *The strategy leader should act as scribe*
This has a number of benefits. Firstly, this ensures that the writing is consistently clear and legible. Secondly, it allows the strategy leader to act as editor and quality controller.

72 *Clarify and simplify the idea descriptions when appropriate...*
This is of primary importance for ensuring consistent high quality of the ideas. It puts a heavy responsibility on the strategy leader, but he/she is there to be more than just a dumb recorder after all!

73 *... but don't overdo it or the process will drag on*
This means carefully limiting any interventions based on fine judgement. As a general rule, do not intervene on more than 20% of the ideas or you will hinder the forward momentum and you may also dilute ownership.

74 *Call a further two minutes' private thought midway*
This helps to refuel the creative energies, freshens an ailing process, and rebuilds a sense of dramatic tension.

75 *Try to identify obvious gaps and challenge the participants to fill these*
This again relies on keen judgement from the strategy leader. The choreographed pauses are the obvious times to focus on this (but generally try and do this three or four times on an ad hoc basis).

76 *Keep it moving – don't allow things to get bogged down*
This means injecting a sense of energy (and even mild urgency) at the natural dips in levels of activity that occur.

77 *When momentum recedes, ask for 2 more ideas then close the session*
Too early is better than too late (you can always add more ideas later).

BREAK-OUT BRAINSTORM

The break-out brainstorm involves splitting a large group into sub-groups, each of which focuses on a different perspective of the strategic challenge. The whole team recombines to review and refine the outputs. This works well when participants have a functional, product line or regional perspective to bring to the central strategic question. This is a much more dynamic and interactive brainstorming technique than the formal brainstorm. It can therefore lead to depth as well as breadth of responses.

Ideal Application
- Groups of >10
- Depth and breadth
- Cross-functional / multi-regional perspectives

Participants
- Group splits into subgroups which each focus on a different perspective
- Subgroups discuss ideas and capture the good ones on post its
- Post its are displayed on a structured wallchart
- Whole group recombines to review and refine all ideas contributed

Strategy Leader
- Clarifies the exact question being asked and the subgroup perspectives
- Provides checklists for each subgroup as guidance
- Spends time with each subgroup at the outset to help get them started
- Returns to each subgroup to coach and challenge
- Reconvenes the combined group when sufficient ground is covered
- Facilitates discussion and refinement of each subgroup's contribution

Output

A
B
C
D
E

10-20 good ideas for each subtopic

Duration
- 45 mins in subgroups
- 90 minutes in plenary review

Overview of technique

The break-out brainstorm technique is illustrated above. This example shows fifteen participants split into five groups of three. Each sub-group A to E is focusing on a different perspective. For example, this might cover business functions: sales, R&D, operations, service and finance. Alternatively, the sub-groups might cover different geographic or product line perspectives (or a combination of all of these).

How it works

Stage 1 – Idea Creation by Break-out Group

This technique comprises two stages – the initial break-out sessions followed by a plenary review of the findings. In stage 1, the sub-groups work for around 30–45 minutes discussing ideas and capturing the good ones on post-its, which are then displayed on a single wall-chart. The strategy leader spends time with each sub-group and provides each with a tailored checklist as guidance on the scope of their perspective. The strategy leader helps each sub-group to get going, and returns to provide coaching and challenge on the emerging outputs. After the initial 30 minutes, when the sub-groups have displayed at least 10–15 good ideas on the wall-chart, the strategy leader reconvenes the combined group to review the respective outputs as a second stage in the process.

Stage 2 – Plenary Review and Refinement

Stage 2 requires rapid review of each post-it by 'layer' of the wall-chart in a systematic fashion involving the complete workshop team. This is an important opportunity for clarification, cross-fertilisation and enhancement and the strategy leader should encourage open discussion (but should also limit this to comments that add value and should make sure that momentum is maintained). This review stage should lead to alterations to existing ideas as well as new post-its for new ideas raised. The second stage typically takes 60–90 minutes (sometimes more) and is an important opportunity to improve the break-out inputs. The typical deliverable is a multi-layered wall-chart displaying up to 100 good ideas. These ideas have the benefit of functional expertise as well as cross-functional challenge and refinements.

Typical Duration

135 mins	The total time required for a break-out brainstorm is 135 minutes – 45 minutes for the initial sub-group work followed by 90 minutes to review and enhance the total outputs in the combined group.

Advantages	Disadvantages
• This approach can lead to more in-depth consideration of ideas and tends to yield a higher quality result compared with a formal brainstorm. • For the first stage, the break-out topics and sub-groups are designed to align with the different responsibilities of the participants. This ensures qualified and credible initial contributions based on specific knowledge and expertise. • For the second stage, there is an opportunity for cross-fertilisation and enhancement which leads to a more joined-up and robust output. • Everyone feels ownership of the combined outputs which have enhanced depth as well as breadth.	• This approach is not suitable for smaller groups (less than 9) as each sub-group ideally needs 3 or more participants to work effectively. • This is a less 'controlled' format compared with the formal brainstorm. It requires more work from the strategy leader to make sure that each sub-group is working to scope and that no individual is dominating. • There is less opportunity for 'editorial control' of the outputs by the strategy leader (but with the right team this might not be needed). • The second review stage can drag on and needs to be constantly and carefully ushered along to a conclusion.

Ideal application

The break-out brainstorm should be considered as an alternative to formal brainstorming, particularly with large, diverse groups, in early stages of concept development. It works particularly well in large, cross-functional or multi-regional groups where the break-out basis can be aligned with the various areas of expertise within the group. It tends to apply well in projects set in large, matrix type organisations.

Practical Tips – Leading Break-out Brainstorms

78 **Prepare checklists for each sub-group as guidance on scope**
This is important as the sub-groups are mostly self-managing and it is crucial that they don't drift off-message.

79 **Include the specific question being asked on the checklist**
Never underestimate the potential for people to try to answer a different question!

80 **Make sure the capture of ideas on post-its is meaningful and legible**
Short descriptive phrases are ideal for post-its – single words do not say enough and long sentences are not easily digestible. Provide a clear guide and show some examples.

81 **Consider nominating a leader for each sub-group**
This makes sense if there is a natural leader, but self-managing is also fine if you wish to avoid any hierarchy.

82 **Keep the sub-groups in the same room**
The buzz of multiple discussions creates a helpful, creative, energised dynamic if carried out in the same room. Also, moving everyone into different areas wastes valuable time.

83 **Check soon after launch that all groups are on the right track**
Visit each of the sub-groups quickly. Aim to spend just 2 minutes with each group to guide their early thoughts.

84 **Use a second coaching session to challenge and identify possible gaps**
Spend a bit longer on the second coaching round but remember that with 45 minutes and 5 sub-groups you only have 9 minutes per group for both coaching sessions.

85 **Make sure the wall-chart is the right size!**
This sounds trivial but it is worth that little bit of extra forethought to make sure that the visible output is as organised and clean as possible. A typical wall-chart can be made from 4 or 8 flipchart sheets taped together.

86 **For the stage 2 review, keep discussion short and to the point**
It is important to cover every idea on the wall-chart – even if this is just reading it out and acknowledging its relevance. Make sure this moves very quickly – only allow detailed discussion when it is really justified.

87 **Get the originators of stage 2 ideas to record these on new post-its**
This helps with time management (they do this while you move onto the next idea) but also ensures ownership.

88 **Summarise the general themes emerging at the end of the session**
A typical output can be overpowering in terms of detail. Before closing the session, help everyone to see the 'wood from the trees' by summarising the major emerging themes.

CAROUSEL BRAINSTORM

The carousel brainstorm is appropriate in the latter stages of a workshop where one or more cycles of creativity and analysis has already been undertaken. It is typically used to identify the next steps required. It can be a dynamic and inclusive process just when energies are at a low point. It can also help to ensure that the workshop closes on a high note.

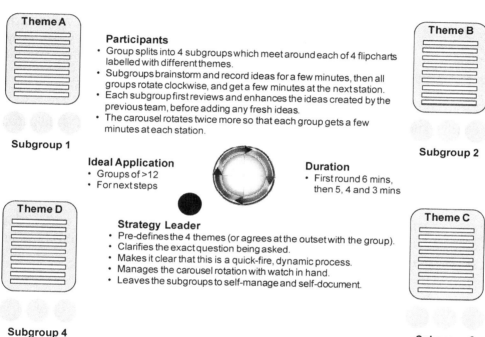

Theme A

Subgroup 1

Theme B

Subgroup 2

Theme D

Subgroup 4

Theme C

Subgroup 3

Participants
- Group splits into 4 subgroups which meet around each of 4 flipcharts labelled with different themes.
- Subgroups brainstorm and record ideas for a few minutes, then all groups rotate clockwise, and get a few minutes at the next station.
- Each subgroup first reviews and enhances the ideas created by the previous team, before adding any fresh ideas.
- The carousel rotates twice more so that each group gets a few minutes at each station.

Ideal Application
- Groups of >12
- For next steps

Duration
- First round 6 mins, then 5, 4 and 3 mins

Strategy Leader
- Pre-defines the 4 themes (or agrees at the outset with the group).
- Clarifies the exact question being asked.
- Makes it clear that this is a quick-fire, dynamic process.
- Manages the carousel rotation with watch in hand.
- Leaves the subgroups to self-manage and self-document.

Overview of technique

The carousel brainstorm technique is illustrated above. It is important to explain that this works best as a quick-fire, dynamic process which requires a final surge of energy from the participants – typically at the end of an intense workshop. The aim is to identify next steps around a small number of key themes (four themes are used here by way of example). The themes tend to align with the key strategic thrusts that have emerged during the workshop and require crystallising by the strategy leader. For example, in the *Global Production Strategy* case study described earlier, the key themes were *Outsourcing, Network Consolidation, New Market Entry* and *Competence Development*.

How it works

The themes are written as titles on 4 separate flipchart pads which are stationed at the four corners of the room. The team is then split into 4 sub-groups – each sub-group will be getting a few minutes at each station in turn to contribute to an accumulating set of ideas. This is managed as a rotating 'carousel' (hence the name). The sub-groups move separately to cover each station and get a few minutes to discuss and record ideas on the flipchart. On the instruction of the strategy leader, they then rotate clockwise to get a few minutes at the next station. When each team arrives at a new station, they first have to review the ideas already logged by the previous group (and they are empowered to enhance these if relevant). The group then needs to create and add additional ideas.

The carousel rotates three times in total so that each group gets a few minutes at each station. The time allowed at each stop is deliberately reduced – 6 minutes at the first, 5 at the second, then 4, then 3. This is because the opportunity for incremental improvements is steadily reducing as the lists of ideas expand and mature. The reduced time also instils a sense of urgency and helps to 'raise the game' of tired-out workshop participants.

The output from a carousel brainstorm is typically 15 or so ideas at each station. This combined output can then be prioritised using one of the evaluation techniques (see next section).

Typical Duration	
45 mins	A good time to allow for a carousel brainstorm is 45 minutes. This allows for set-up, the four ideas sessions, and some time for reviewing the outputs.

Advantages	Disadvantages
• The perfect upbeat process for ending an intense, tiring workshop on a high note. This is a fun and hectic group activity. • Produces a wide range of ideas and ensures that everyone has contributed. • Helps everyone get those niggling fears and concerns off their chest – this often forms a rudimentary risk analysis against the emerging strategy. • Clarifies what needs doing as soon as everyone gets back to the day-job so that momentum is not lost. • Instils strong ownership of the outputs.	• This approach is not suitable for smaller groups (less than 9) as each sub-group ideally needs 3 or more participants to work effectively (and the minimum number of themes is 3). • This is not a process for developing depth of thought – it is designed to capture immediate, instinctive responses. • The outputs are typically a bit messy due to different writing styles and the rapid pace.

Ideal application

The carousel brainstorm is not a substitute for the formal or break-out brainstorms as it is not suitable for the initial creative process within concept development. Its ideal application is at the end of workshops where next steps need identifying. It works well with large, diverse groups.

Practical Tips – Leading Carousel Brainstorms

89 **Test your choice of themes with senior participants in advance**
The themes will have become apparent as the emerging strategy matures towards the end of the workshop. However, it is worth checking these with senior stakeholders as early as is practical.

90 **Plan a break directly before the session to prepare the room**
It is important to set this up carefully without the pressures of being 'on stage'. A 15–minute coffee break is enough time to set out the flipcharts and write the theme titles on each.

91 **Make sure that there is enough space in the room**
This requires 4 flipchart stands in the 4 corners of the room. There needs to be sufficient space around each flipchart to comfortably accommodate each sub-group. There also needs to be sufficient access for the sub-groups to move quickly to the next station.

92 **Number off the participants to quickly identify random sub-groups**
For 4 sub-groups this means counting 1, 2, 3, 4, 1, 2, 3, 4 etc while pointing at each individual so that each person knows their number. Group 1 is then all the 1s and so on. Simple – but important to do quickly and crisply.

93 **Make it clear this is quick-fire and ask for a final surge of energy**
This is a bit like a coach's team talk for the last few minutes of a long game. Explain exactly what you need.

94 **Start the first session like a race – ready, steady, go – with watch in hand**
This little bit of drama sets the tone (but also you will need the watch to time the sessions!).

95 **Check with each sub-group at kick-off to make sure that they are on track**
Any intervention has to be extremely short and direct. Observe first and only intervene if the team is clearly off track. Remember that this process aims to capture instinctive responses so don't interfere too much.

96 **Give a one-minute warning before the end of each rotation**
This ensures that the last few ideas get quickly recorded and that the sub-groups are primed to move on.

97 **Remind everyone to review the existing ideas after each rotation**
This supports enhancement of the ideas, promotes cross-fertilisation, and prevents repetition.

98 **Be a visible and audible presence in shepherding the process**
Some participants can get a little bit disoriented so go round making sure everyone is in the right place doing the right thing.

OPTION OR SCENARIO DEVELOPMENT

Strategy projects typically involve the development of different future options or scenarios. This generally follows brainstorming and strategic concept development and is the basis for understanding the future strategic end-state. Break-out groups are ideal for this. The guidelines below focus on option development and scenario development separately, and use case illustrations for clarity.

Title of strategic option: Short, 3 or 4 word title	
Description of option: Short definition of what the option covers (and what it does not cover)	**Key enabling steps:** What is required to make this happen with approximate timescales
Value proposition: Description of how this option creates value for the business	**Implementation team:** Who will drive the delivery of this option
Target markets: Definition of typical target markets with quantification where possible	**Additional sales & profit:** Estimate of potential target sales and profit from this option in 5 years time
Capability needs: Internal skills and competences required to deliver the strategic option	**Development costs:** Estimate of capital and revenue costs for developing this strategic option

Option development

This process involves break-out groups defining a range of strategic future options e.g. new product ideas. This activity is best suited to a small focused group which helps to drive some depth of insight. It requires a structured template to guide each team and to ensure consistency (see illustration above). This enables an initial definition of each strategic option, how it creates value, what is required to make it happen and some rough quantification of the cost/benefit performance. The emphasis here is on simplicity. This creates what is also known as a 'mini-business case'. It aims to be simple at this stage and will require follow-up analysis for validation.

CASE STUDY – **Technology Strategy**

The *Technology Strategy* case study is a good example to illustrate the option development process. To recap, this involved a small, specialist audio equipment supplier with around $30m annual turnover and 200 staff. The aim of the project was to develop a 3-year strategy for R&D investment in new product and service technology. This involved a workshop team of 12 cross-functional representatives with a 2-day pilot workshop followed by a 1-day finalisation workshop four weeks later. The pilot workshop kicked off with a brainstorm of key trends and drivers on the business, which were prioritised to form a set of critical success factors (CSFs). A further brainstorm was held to define potential strategic options, and these were evaluated regarding their fit with the CSFs to create a shortlist of 8 options as shown below.

#	Option title	Votes
1	iPod dock	12
2	Turntable	9
3	Web-based services	9
4	Technology licensing	7
5	Lifestyle services	6
6	Wireless speakers	5
7	Music centre	5
8	Multi-room system	5

These strategic options were a mix of new product opportunities (iPod dock, turntable, wireless speakers), a move towards more of a 'system' approach (music centre and multi-room audio system) as well as a more ambitious thrust into different business models (service-based offerings and technology licensing). The options had been prioritised by the group (using the simple 'dot' voting method described in the following section) with the results as shown (with highest priority towards the top of the list). The next challenge was to understand at an initial level of detail exactly what these options meant by creating a specification and mini-business case. The objective was to qualify the attractiveness of the strategic options (but not to attempt to get into too much detail which would be better covered in a follow-on activity).

To develop the options, the 12 workshop participants were split into 4 break-out groups of 3 each. The 8 strategic options that had emerged from the initial brainstorm work were allocated 2 per group (with each group getting a higher and a lower priority option). The groups were given 90 minutes (45 minutes per option) to develop the initial definitions. Each group then presented the outputs back to the combined group for discussion and refinement. The deliverable from this activity was 8 draft definitions of strategic options in a consistent format including some rough quantification of costs and benefits. These were in a suitable form for ongoing evaluation and further detailing (which is covered in the following section on Evaluation Techniques).

Scenario development

Scenarios differ from options in that they focus on different future end states rather than different product, technology or market opportunities. The approach for scenarios is similar to options in the use of a structured, pre-defined template to guide small, focused break-out teams. Careful preparation is required to design the dimensions of the template, which requires significant tailoring to the context.

CASE STUDY – Global Production Strategy

The *Global Production Strategy* project is used as an illustration. To recap, the aim was to define the long-term vision for the global production footprint. This initially involved pilot workshops covering each global product line. Each pilot consisted of various brainstorming and evaluation activities to define the underpinning strategic concepts. The next activity involved the creation of different future scenarios for the production network.

Scenario Title: Short, 3 or 4 word title

Value Proposition: Short description of how this scenario creates value for the business

Markets / Plant type	EAME	Americas	Asia
Volume Assembly	Plant location		
Agile Assembly			
Contract Assembly			
Volume Components			
Agile Components			
Finishing Warehouse			

Here the template shown above drove the choices for locating different plant types for serving the three major regional markets. The combination of a structured grid with a graphical representation helped clarify the details whilst ensuring ease of communication. The 15 workshop participants were split into 3 sub-groups and each developed 3 different scenarios based on different themes. These were then reviewed and consolidated to form a broad range of alternatives that could be evaluated and refined.

Typical Duration

150 mins

A good time to allow for an option/scenario development session is 150 minutes. This is enough to cover several options or scenarios at an initial level of detail (remembering that further detail is best carried out later on after the workshop).

Advantages	Disadvantages
• Option or scenario development is the ideal method for adding 'flesh' to the 'bones' of a strategy. The 'bones' emerge from initial brainstorming and strategic analysis. The 'flesh' of options or scenarios starts to turn concept into reality. • The optimum size of the break-out groups is 3–8. More than this can get unmanageable. More break-out groups will provide a broader set of alternatives and, even if these overlap, it will help make sure the full breadth of possibility has been covered.	• There are no inherent disadvantages in using this approach in workshops as it is a central part of the strategic process. • Where this approach does not work effectively, it is generally due to insufficient preparation in terms of the underpinning strategic concepts and the design of the templates.

Ideal application

Option or scenario development should be included in most creative strategy workshops to build on the initial concepts and to start to crystallise the strategic vision. It is the vehicle for translating strategic principles into understanding what the future looks like, and leading onto how we might get there.

Practical Tips – Leading Option/Scenario Development Sessions

99 **Get the right level of detail in the templates**
Too much detail required in the templates can overwhelm the sub-group but too little will yield a trivial or meaningless output. The terms 'mini-business case' and 'elevator pitch' are helpful here. We want to be able to describe the strategic option simply but effectively using a number of key dimensions.

100 **Mix qualitative and quantitative elements in the template**
A combination of words and numbers is ideal in articulating the essence of a strategic option. These work hand-in-hand, e.g. estimating quantified benefits will often help to qualify exactly what we mean in our wording.

101 **Design break-out groups around the skills and champions available**
This is a delicate balance but the emphasis should be on including those who are knowledgeable and those likely to drive implementation. Two primary benefits of strategy workshops are consultation and ownership.

102 **Know when to have self-facilitating sub-groups**
Sub-groups of 3 or 4, where the template is relatively straightforward, works well with self-facilitation (with perhaps two short coaching sessions). Larger sub-groups with more complex tasks generally benefit from one strategy leader per group.

103 **Use PowerPoint for facilitated sub-groups, wall-charts for self-facilitated**
Both media work well with option/scenario development. One rule of thumb is to use wall-charts with small self-facilitating sub-groups, and projected PowerPoint for larger, facilitated sub-groups to maintain a clear point of focus.

104 **Expect the options or scenarios to evolve**
Some options coming out of these break-out sessions may look quite different from those that were planned and expected going in. This is not necessarily a problem as this is essentially an iterative process where the deliverables are maturing at every stage. Allow flexibility in the formats to enable this ongoing evolution.

105 **Strictly limit mutual feedback time**
The great temptation is to try to solve any issues that arise during feedback and questions but this can soon lead to a level of detail that is not appropriate for a workshop. Make sure issues are recorded for future investigation and then move on.

106 **Consider weighted criteria scoring as a next step**
This naturally follows the initial development of options/scenarios and is covered in the next main section on Evaluation Techniques.

STORYBOARDING

Storyboarding is a term used to describe implementation planning at a course level of detail. This technique tends to apply to the middle stages of a strategy process when focus switches from strategic concept and option/scenario development to understanding 'how to make it happen'. It generally captures key actions on an annual or quarterly level of detail. Importantly, it can also capture other key elements of the 'story' including costs, benefits, risk etc.

	Year 1	Year 2	Year 3	Year 4	Year 5
New customer initiatives	• Bullet point summary	• Bullet point summary	• Bullet point summary	• Bullet point summary	• Bullet point summary
Product launches	• Bullet point summary	• Bullet point summary	• Bullet point summary	• Bullet point summary	• Bullet point summary
Enabling changes in the organisation	• Bullet point summary	• Bullet point summary	• Bullet point summary	• Bullet point summary	• Bullet point summary
Investment in this year	$m	$m	$m	$m	$m
Revenue growth	$m	$m	$m	$m	$m
Profit growth	$m	$m	$m	$m	$m
Risk areas	description	description	description	description	description

Overview of technique

Storyboarding involves break-out teams filling out structured templates of the form illustrated above. Option and scenario storyboarding are described separately below.

Storyboarding a set of options

One key advantage of storyboarding is that it builds directly on the preceding work on option or scenario development. For options, storyboarding requires the sequencing of the implementation of each option over time in a logical way. This requires use of the option descriptions and financial evaluation as previously defined, and relies on some practical judgement and common sense to assess what is achievable. It is often appropriate to create alternative storyboards to reflect, for example, a conservative approach, an ambitious approach and an aggressive approach. These can be pre-defined as different missions for 3 separate sub-groups, or each sub-group can be asked to consider all of these themes to create multiple storyboards.

A typical template used for option storyboarding is shown above. This has a simple year-by-year structure, capturing the key strategic changes (customer initiatives, product launches, enabling changes in the organisation), estimating the financial impact of the changes (sales and profit growth, investment), and describing the key risks (e.g. likely competitive reaction).

Storyboarding alternative scenarios

For scenarios, storyboarding is best used for understanding the implementation sequence for each particular scenario (or the most attractive ones). Here the scenario has defined an ideal end-state, and the storyboard is used to understand how to get there. This builds on the scenario descriptions previously created to lay out the logical sequence of steps that will deliver the end state. As with options, break-out groups can be given different missions in terms of level of ambition. There may also be different paths for reaching the same end-state which can be defined using different storyboards for the same scenario.

CASE STUDY – **Diversification Strategy**

Returning to the case of the *Diversification Strategy* project, storyboarding was used during the latter stages of the pilot workshop to understand the macro-level implementation plan and its effect on the business. To recap, this involved a specialist, value-added reseller supplying and maintaining equipment used by major food retailers (tills, handheld devices etc). The project objective was to develop a diversification strategy in terms of new markets and products to reduce exposure to one major client (while retaining this client as a valuable co-development partner). Initial brainstorming during the workshop defined the key trends and drivers on the business followed by a set of strategic options which were prioritised and then developed. The next challenge was to create a 'storyboard' for each high priority option to show how it might be implemented over time, also considering the likely financial impact on the business.

	Year 1	Year 2	Year 3	Year 4	Year 5
Key actions	• Develop marketing materials aimed at DIY segment	• Launch basic products in DIY	• Launch DIY service agreements	• Launch advanced products in DIY segment	• Launch advanced DIY service agreements
Enabling changes	• Recruit DIY marketing champion	• Recruit DIY sales champion	• Recruit DIY service team	-	• Grow service team
Investment	$100k	$100k	$100k	$20k	$100k
Revenue growth	-	$200k	$1m	$2m	$4m
Profit growth	-	$20k	$150k	$300k	$600k
Risk areas	• Continuing gravitational pull of food customers	• Possible competitive reaction	• Potential for over-commitment on service levels	• Possible warranty exposure in harsher environment	• Potential for over-commitment on service levels

One important option that arose was to enter DIY as a totally new retail segment alongside food. The storyboard for this is shown here. This considered the key steps required to realise this strategic option on a year-by-year basis over 5 years. This included estimates of investment costs, revenue growth and profit growth.

The storyboarding process helped the team to think through logical steps to prepare and launch products, and then services, into this new area of business. Many of the standard products were suitable, and there was also a need for more advanced service agreements in this market. There were risks involved, however, including competitive reaction and exposure to warranty claims in a harsher operating environment. The storyboard captured the key steps together with estimates for investment, revenue growth and profit growth. Overall, this activity helped to confirm this option as an attractive and practical strategic thrust.

Typical Duration

90 mins	A good time to allow for a storyboarding session is 90 minutes. This is enough to cover an initial level of detail (remembering that further detail may be covered by a subsequent action planning session).

Advantages	Disadvantages
• Storyboarding is the perfect 'reality check' on an emerging strategy. It forces workshop participants to consider the practical implementation steps. • Simple storyboarding templates help drive clarity of thinking and visualisation of the necessary actions and associated impact. • Storyboards build directly on the detailed concepts, options and scenarios already established, and integrate these into a relevant and digestible format. • Storyboards link directly with discounted cash-flow analysis by estimating the key costs and benefits, and defining their timing on an annual basis. They also help to illustrate the assumptions behind financial analysis for ongoing challenge.	• The level of detail possible in storyboarding is limited. This is a broad-brush tool for understanding possible routes for strategy implementation. It does not produce a detailed implementation plan (which requires further work within and following the workshop). • Storyboarding different options using separate subgroups can create over-ambitious plans if the cumulative effect on limited resources is not considered. It is worth aggregating and adjusting the storyboards as a second stage activity. This is an opportunity to re-phase key steps to account for availability of funds or human resources.

Ideal application

Storyboarding is best used as the bridge between theoretical concepts and practical reality. It is therefore ideally positioned towards the end of a pilot workshop. It naturally tests some of the assumptions and theories developed in the preceding activities, and often results in the refinement and clarification of the underpinning strategic principles.

Practical Tips – Leading Storyboarding Sessions

107 — **Pre-define the linkage between options/scenarios and the storyboard**
It makes sense for there to be common elements between the option/scenario templates and the storyboard template. The storyboard is really a time-based view of a more detailed set of information. For example, if profit growth is a key objective, the initial option template may require an initial estimate of the profit potential. The storyboard template should then show how the profit potential might grow over time, also including the phasing of the required investments.

108 — **Get the right level of detail**
For the horizontal time axis of a storyboard, year-by-year tends to be workable; quarter-by-quarter is sometimes relevant (especially in the nearer term); month-by-month is probably too specific and you will get lost in detail. For the vertical axis, the elements here need to fit the central project theme and the emerging strategic concepts. The topics tend to be fairly broad in definition to allow some freedom of interpretation. The overall template should ideally fit on a single PowerPoint slide and be legible when projected on a screen so this limits the amount of detail that is practical.

109 — **Mix qualitative and quantitative elements within the storyboard**
As with the option template, it is useful to mix descriptive statements with quantified estimates of the business impact. The quantified elements are approximate only but thinking through the quantification often helps to provide a common sense check on the descriptive elements (and the underlying strategic logic).

110 — **Aim to have self-facilitating sub-groups**
Storyboarding is relatively straightforward and usually works well with self-facilitated break-out groups. Larger groups or groups with significant political tensions are more likely to need facilitation.

111 — **PowerPoint is marginally preferred over wall-charts for the templates**
Both work well with storyboarding. One obvious advantage with PowerPoint is that it is easily edited during feedback discussions.

112 — **Capture any necessary changes to options and scenarios that emerge**
The discipline of thinking through how to make the strategy happen usually prompts subtle adjustments to the strategic elements already defined. Adjustments should be captured before they are lost. This is easily achieved where the previous outputs have been displayed as wall-charts by adding meaningful post-its.

113 — **Set different missions for each group to cover the full spectrum**
The approach of setting different levels of ambition for each break-out group works well. Another option is to refer back to the trends and drivers on the business and ask each group to consider different market or macroeconomic assumptions for their respective tasks.

ACTION PLANNING

Action planning operates at a finer level of detail than storyboarding, and usually covers a shorter time frame (e.g. Year 1 rather than 5 years). It is often performed on the major foundation and enabling projects in the finalisation stages of strategy development. This activity tends to focus on more detailed tasks and on the major questions of what, why, who and when i.e. what the task is, why we are doing it, who is responsible, when does it need to happen.

Project Title: *3 or 4 word title*					
#	Title	Action description	Desired outcome	Who's involved	Timing
1	*3 or 4 word title*	*Short descriptive sentences to define what needs to happen*	*Deliverables of the action (with tangible impact)*	*Who's responsible for delivery, who supports*	*Start & finish*
2					
3					
4					
5					
6					
7					
8					
9					
10					

Overview of technique

Action planning involves break-out teams filling out structured templates of the form illustrated above. The objective is to develop implementation project plans in an initial stage of detail, getting input from a range of interested parties and building ownership and accountability.

Using action planning in the closing stages of workshops

Action planning is probably the easiest workshop technique to apply as the objective and approach are simple and intuitive. However, it can be a crucial part of the closing stages of a workshop as it helps define the ongoing actions and accountabilities and ensures continued momentum.

Defining the foundation and enabling projects

One important linking step between storyboarding and action planning is the definition of the foundation and enabling projects. This may be obvious based on the elements of the storyboard (or the preceding options). For example, the foundation projects for the *Diversification Strategy* included the launch of a new product, the launch of a new service, the development of sales with three new customers, and entering the DIY segment. The enabling projects included the implementation of improved internal contract control procedures. These projects all emerged directly from the option development and storyboarding outputs but it is worth noting here that the third project – development of sales with three new customers – was actually three separate options bundled together. This simple example illustrates the important principle that some judgement is required in designing the implementation projects in order to group options that naturally fit together and to align them with the functional responsibilities within the business.

Break-outs using action planning templates

Once the foundation and enabling projects have been determined, break-out teams can be deployed to work against a simple template to define the activities, resources, responsibilities, timescales etc. A typical action planning template is shown on the previous page. The simple structure helps the team to think through the implementation activities in a logical sequence and to understand who will deliver them and when this needs to happen. This only provides a rudimentary action plan at this stage which is then suitable for validation and refinement after the workshop.

Typical Duration	
90 mins	A good time to allow for an action planning session is 90 minutes. This is enough to cover an initial level of detail (remembering that further detail is best carried out later on after the workshop).

Advantages	Disadvantages
• Action planning is an important final stage in strategy workshops. It builds on the preceding strategy definition and links directly with implementation. • Action planning helps to confirm the practicality of the strategy by showing how it can work in practice. • This approach works well in small break-out groups and can help drive ownership of the ongoing plan (if the implementation champions are directly involved). • The approach is simple and intuitive and easily facilitated.	• Whilst action planning goes into more detail than storyboarding, the output is still not presentable as a detailed implementation plan. This will require focused follow-on work by the core project team after the workshop. • As with storyboarding, if separate action plans are developed by separate sub-groups, they can prove over-ambitious by under-estimating the combined impact on resources. It is therefore worth carrying out a follow-on activity to aggregate the action plans and phase timings accordingly to match resource availability.

Ideal application

Action planning is a crucial stage towards the end of the strategy development cycle and tends to be used in finalisation workshops. It is ideally carried out against the key foundation and enabling projects that make up the strategy implementation.

Note: It is worth explaining the difference here between action planning and a carousel brainstorm regarding closing a workshop. Action planning is generally used for planning the strategic projects that will deliver the strategy. Carousel brainstorming is generally used to define the next steps required to complete the strategy development process itself.

Practical Tips – Leading Action Planning Sessions

114

Check the foundation/enabling project titles with senior participants
As described, defining the project titles may require some subtle bundling or adjustment to the strategic options or storyboard elements already defined. It is worth planning a meal or coffee break to gather thoughts on this and to test with a subset of senior participants.

115

Carefully design the break-out teams
This can also be tackled during a coffee break but you might consider second-guessing the likely projects and break-out team make-up further in advance. This will undoubtedly change but this will help reduce the task to a simple adjustment rather than a 'design-from-scratch' exercise. Remember that this is now the late stages of what is likely to have been a pretty gruelling workshop and everyone will be tired.

116

Don't spend too long – this is still broad-brush planning
Effective action plans can generally be developed in 90 minutes or less. Make it clear that you are not looking for minute details and check in with each group early on to reinforce this.

117

Create healthy competition between sub-groups on level of ambition
It is often a useful by-product of workshop break-out activities that the teams compete to provide the best outputs. Try and encourage this with some well-judged suggestions and comparisons.

118

Rotate the 'internal customers' between the sub-groups to challenge
This works well at this stage where the executable projects are defined and it is clear who the internal suppliers and customers are.

119

Make the preceding outputs available to each group for reference
This seems obvious but it is not always easily achieved. If these elements have already been captured in PowerPoint then it means a simple print-and-distribute task. If these are on wall-charts, then you may need to move the right charts into each break-out room. The challenge comes where major wall-charts have data needed by more than one group. The best solution here is to get each group to note down the important elements before the session commences for ease of reference during the session.

120

PowerPoint is marginally preferred to wall-charts for the templates
Both work well with action planning but here I would tend towards PowerPoint as there is a bit more detail to capture and this supports a more flexible and neater result which can be adjusted live.

E

SIX EVALUATION TECHNIQUES FOR WORKSHOPS

Overview
Dot Prioritisation
Clustering
Gallery Walk & Issue Capture
Weighted Criteria Scoring
2x2 Matrices / Bubble Charts
Traffic Light Analysis

OVERVIEW

Strategy workshops involve cycles of divergent, creative thinking and convergent, analytical thinking. This section describes a range of useful analytical evaluation techniques that provide the basis for comparing and assessing the various ideas, concepts, options and scenarios that are created. These techniques also provide a rational framework that can disperse the emotional and political tensions that inevitably arise during group activities. These are therefore vital tools for herding the wild cats.

Evaluation techniques help to sort the good ideas from the not so good

Various evaluation techniques

Evaluating large amounts of information and helping participants to 'see the wood from the trees' are essential parts of leading strategy workshops. The techniques available range from the extremely simple but powerful 'dot prioritisation' technique to more sophisticated weighted scoring methods and use of Excel charts. The trick is knowing when to use which technique. A selection of tried and tested techniques is introduced below, and each is then described in more detail through this section.

Technique	Description	Ideal use
Dot prioritisation	• Participants allocate sticky dots to the best ideas • Open and democratic in nature • Based on expert judgement rather than hard facts	For filtering a large volume of ideas after brainstorming
Clustering	• For grouping similar or linked ideas • Participants physically move post-its into groups • Best done without conferring • Cluster titles can be pre-set or allowed to emerge • Often performed after dot prioritisation	For improving the manageability of a formal brainstorm output
Gallery walk & issue capture	• Helps large groups to assimilate a large amount of data and define issues/gaps • With wall-charts arranged in stations, sub-groups spend time at each station in turn • Enables high quality, focused discussion	For reviewing draft strategies at aggregation and finalisation workshops
Weighted criteria scoring	• Assesses options against a balanced set of criteria incorporating differentiated weightings • Criteria include qualitative and quantitative factors • Supports blending of expert judgement and facts	Classic technique for comparing options or scenarios
2x2 matrices & bubble charts	• Assessing options against two key dimensions • Each dimension based on weighted criteria • Provides 2x2 graphical output • Quadrants of the 2x2 often reflect different strategic decision areas or types of options	Useful visualisation technique for assessing options, scenarios and projects
Traffic light analysis	• Simple, 3–level prioritisation of options or risks using red, amber, green as choices • Often used alongside quantitative analysis to assess qualitative factors • Based on expert judgement	Useful visualisation technique for summary-level project evaluation

DOT PRIORITISATION

This is the simplest evaluation tool in the strategy leader's toolbox, but it is an extremely effective way of 'seeing the wood from the trees'. It is typically used to prioritise a large volume of brainstorm ideas to identify a ranked list of the most useful ones. It involves each participant allocating self-adhesive dots to ideas listed on flipcharts or shown on individual post-its. It is democratic in nature – each person gets to cast the same number of votes. It therefore relies on expert opinions rather than hard facts but, even so, with the right balance of workshop participants, this works amazingly well.

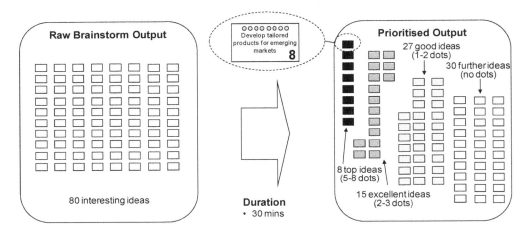

Raw Brainstorm Output

80 interesting ideas

Duration
• 30 mins

Develop tailored products for emerging markets **8**

Prioritised Output

27 good ideas
(1-2 dots)

30 further ideas
(no dots)

8 top ideas
(5-8 dots)

15 excellent ideas
(2-3 dots)

Process
• Strategy Leader provides each participant with a fixed number of small, self-adhesive dots (say 8 dots each).
• Strategy Leader defines prioritisation instruction e.g. allocate dots to the ideas that will create most value.
• Participants stick dots directly onto the post-its for their 8 favourite ideas.
• Strategy Leader counts up the dots on each post-it and writes the number in the corner.

How it works

The most common application of dot prioritisation is following a brainstorming activity. This works well after a formal, break-out or carousel brainstorm, particularly where ideas are recorded on individual post-its or on flipcharts. The process is illustrated in the diagram on the previous page.

This shows the typical output from a brainstorm comprising, say, 80 interesting ideas written on 80 post-its stuck on a single wall-chart. The divergent process of brainstorming has served its purpose perfectly in tapping the combined wisdom of the group in defining a very wide range of possible ideas for strategic action. The problem now is that this mass of information is overpowering, and needs filtering via a convergent process to help sift out the great ideas from the so-so ones. The process here involves providing each workshop participant with a small, limited number of self-adhesive dots (say, 8 dots, typically 8mm in diameter) and asking each person to stick the dots on their 8 favourite ideas. The strategy leader needs to define the basis of prioritisation with a simple statement. For example, 'Select the 8 best ideas that will create most value for the business over the next 5 years.' It works best if the participants work in isolation here (rather than conferring) to prevent any dominant personalities influencing the choice. This is essentially a democratic process – each team member gets 8 votes to cast as they see fit. There is no clever analysis involved: this relies totally on the expert judgement of the team.

The typical output from dot prioritisation is illustrated on the right-hand side of the chart. Here the results have been sorted into 4 priority bands with priority represented by increasing intensity of colour. The top ideas might fall into a band having 5–8 dots, the next level 3–4 dots, next 1–2 dots, leaving a large number of so-so ideas with no dots. The distribution obviously varies depending on the context, and the bands can be tailored to fit. As an alternative to moving the post-its into bands, it is often helpful to transcribe the top scoring ideas onto a flipchart in descending order of score. Via this simple and quick process, we have converted an overpowering mass of thinking into a structured, useful output which is suitable for ongoing creativity and analysis.

Linking dot prioritisation and clustering

Dot prioritisation is often followed by clustering which groups the ideas into similar categories. This improves the manageability of a large volume of ideas and, in turn, links to option/scenario development. Clustering and option/scenario development are covered in the following sections.

Typical Duration

30 mins

The total time required for the dot prioritisation process is around 30 minutes (including counting up the dots and transcribing the top priority ideas to a flipchart).

Advantages	Disadvantages
• Dot prioritisation is ideal for first-stage evaluation. It is simple, quick and effective. • This approach is inherently consultative and participative. It is largely immune to undue influencing by dominant individuals or to fit political positions. • The output is immediately visible and can be used for ongoing activities (such as clustering and strategic option development). • Everyone has an equal stake in the outcome and this builds strong ownership. • It works well with small and large groups.	• Dot prioritisation relies totally on expert opinions and is not based on hard data or factual analysis. • As a consequence, its application should be limited to first-stage or 'rough' prioritisation. • Dot prioritisation needs to be followed by more sophisticated evaluation later in the workshop or after the workshop. (Options for more sophisticated evaluation within workshops include weighted criteria scoring.)

Ideal application

Dot prioritisation is ideally performed after every broad brainstorming activity (formal, break-out or carousel brainstorming) as first-stage prioritisation. It is not suitable following the more structured creative activities of option or scenario development, where more sophisticated evaluation methods such as weighted criteria scoring provide more value.

Practical Tips – Leading Dot Prioritisation Sessions

121 *How to define the right number of dots per participant*
In general, the choice is 6, 8 or 10 dots. 8 is suggested as the default. Use 6 when there are a smaller number of ideas generated (typically with smaller groups) and, conversely, 10 dots for large volumes of ideas with larger groups. The problem associated with too many dots relative to the number of ideas is that nearly every idea gets a vote i.e. the prioritisation effect is dispersed or lacking in definition. Too few dots relative to the number of ideas makes the output look restricted or too narrowly focused.

122 *Don't allow discussion or conferring*
As mentioned, discussion should be discouraged explicitly by the strategy leader to prevent anyone influencing the 'democratic' process.

123 *Make sure the participants have registered and absorbed all the ideas*
This happens naturally during formal brainstorming (where everyone hears every idea at source) and carousel brainstorming (where reviewing ideas from other groups is part of the process) but not necessarily during break-out brainstorming (where the sub-groups work in isolation). For the latter, make sure the whole group quickly reviews all the ideas (led by the strategy leader to ensure time efficiency) before dot prioritisation. Don't assume that everyone will be able to read everyone else's ideas and absorb them without a formal review process.

124 *Don't make this sound more sophisticated than it is*
The workshop will soon lose credibility if this activity is claimed to be based on robust scientific principles. It is a simple tool used appropriately for rough prioritisation.

125 *Use a coffee break to count up the dots and to prepare the result*
It will take 5 minutes or so to count up the dots and write the relevant number on each post-it. Moving the post-its into priority bands takes another 5 minutes. One alternative option to the bands is to transcribe the top 10 or so ideas onto a single flipchart page in decreasing order of dots per idea. It is better to do this in the relative calm of a coffee break (rather than under the impatient supervision of a herd of wild cats).

126 *Ask an assistant to capture the output straight away in Excel*
This takes more than a coffee break but can be done in parallel with other activities. The output can then be clearly displayed and automatically sorted into descending order.

127 *Encourage consideration of other people's ideas (not just one's own)!*
This is a rather impertinent point to make to senior managers but it is clear that some individuals will tend to favour ideas created by them personally or by their break-out group. This does not need any special rules – a slightly tongue-in-cheek request from the strategy leader helps offset the tendency (and can help to inject a lighter, more humorous touch).

CLUSTERING

The second 'rough' technique for processing brainstorm outputs (which often complements dot prioritisation) is clustering. This involves grouping similar or linked ideas into clusters that can then be characterised with meaningful titles. This is best performed after prioritisation and is another way of seeing 'the wood from the trees'. In essence, it reduces complexity: typically, it might condense 80 individual ideas into 8 or so clusters.

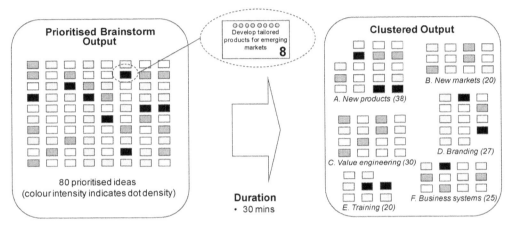

Prioritised Brainstorm Output

80 prioritised ideas
(colour intensity indicates dot density)

Develop tailored products for emerging markets **8**

Duration
- 30 mins

Clustered Output

A. New products (38)
B. New markets (20)
C. Value engineering (30)
D. Branding (27)
E. Training (20)
F. Business systems (25)

Process
- Strategy Leader asks the participants to move post-its into natural groupings.
- No talking or conferring allowed.
- Participants permitted to reallocate each other's moves if they see necessary.
- When clusters start to emerge, facilitator suggests titles for clusters and writes these adjacent to each.
- When clustering is almost complete, facilitator helps finish the process.
- Strategy Leader counts up total dots per cluster to provide cluster prioritisation.

How it works

Clustering simply organises a large volume of ideas into categories. The main challenge with this process is defining the right categories. One option is for the strategy leader to pre-define these but this is not straightforward and can be stressful under workshop conditions. The preferred method is to let the team decide using a 'democratic' approach. The process is illustrated opposite.

Here on the left we have 80 prioritised ideas – 80 individual post-its with dots on each – all stuck on a single, large wall-chart. The 'democratic' process involves empowering the team to physically move the post-its into groupings that seem to make sense. This involves all the participants gathering around the wall-chart and each doing their bit. The key rule is that it has to be done in silence, with no conferring. This way no-one dominates, and the clusters gradually emerge. The second rule is that participants are permitted to reallocate others' moves if they see fit. These rules create a fun dynamic and a slight air of tension which energises the team.

It does not take long for the initial clusters to emerge and for, say, 60% of the post-its to be allocated but then the rate of progress can tend to slow. At this stage, the strategy leader needs to intervene to help speed up the process. This first involves taking the lead on defining the clusters that have emerged. The strategy leader suggests appropriate titles and refines these based on feedback from the group. As each title is agreed, the strategy leader writes the title on the wall-chart adjacent to each cluster. When all titles are settled, it helps if the strategy leader takes control of allocating the final post-its (some of these may end up in a 'miscellaneous' cluster if they don't fit anywhere else).

Prioritising the clusters

Having now grouped the ideas into clusters which have defined labels, it is a straightforward task to prioritise the clusters by simply adding the total dots on all post-its within each cluster. The totals can be added in brackets after each cluster title.

Typical Duration	
30 mins	The total time required for the clustering process is around 30 minutes (including allocating the titles to the clusters).

Advantages	Disadvantages
• Clustering is a great tool for reducing complexity. The human brain is easily swamped by having to consider 80 different individual ideas but it can easily cope with 8 categories of ideas. • This is a fun and dynamic process which gets the team on their feet and energised. • Leaving the team to define the clusters (rather than trying to pre-define or force-fit them) is more effective and builds ownership of the result.	• This process is clearly not very scientific and the emerging clusters may not be exactly the right ones. This does not matter if it is accepted that this is a fairly rough tool to help digest a large set of ideas. Typically the output is used to drive strategic option development where the ideas and clusters are translated into actionable projects (so this provides a further opportunity for refinement). • This process does require some keen judgement on the part of the strategy leader regarding when and how to intervene.

Ideal application

Formal brainstorming, dot prioritisation and clustering go naturally together as a set. The brainstorm creates a comprehensive (but overwhelming) set of ideas, dot prioritisation ranks them, clustering arranges them into a manageable set of categories. This 3–stage activity is useful early on in the creative process for helping to assimilate a large volume of ideas. The output provides an excellent basis for considering strategic options and future scenarios.

Practical Tips – Leading Clustering Sessions

128 **Make it clear that this is fairly rough but also a bit of fun**
As with dot prioritisation, do not leave it open to doubt as to whether this is a scientific process. Make the team aware that this is a rough evaluation tool that is appropriate for use in this early stage for processing the wealth of ideas that they have generated.

129 **Don't be tempted to intervene too early**
The clustering process usually kicks off with an awkward silence as the team tries to get to grips with the task. Be patient – someone will soon jump in and start moving post-its then others will follow.

130 **Observe closely and start to think of possible cluster titles**
For the first 10–15 minutes, just stand back and observe how the clusters are developing and mentally note the possible titles.

131 **Intervene as soon as the emerging clusters are clear**
This usually happens after 10–15 minutes with, say, 60% of the post-its moved into groupings. Step in now and go around the clusters one-by-one, suggesting the titles and seeking input and agreement from the team. When you have agreement, write the title next to the cluster.

132 **Following the first intervention, become part of the team**
With the clusters defined, encourage the others to continue the process but also become part of the team to help accelerate completion of the task.

133 **Re-title clusters if necessary**
As more post-its are allocated to groupings, it is sometimes appropriate to adjust the titles to fit a slightly broader definition.

134 **Take editorial control towards the end of the process**
The last few post-its tend to be the most difficult to allocate so this requires intervention from the strategy leader.

135 **Create a 'miscellaneous' cluster for the misfits**
One useful technique to finish off the process is to create a miscellaneous cluster to capture any post-its that do not seem to fit anywhere else.

136 **Consider documenting the result live in Excel**
If an assistant has been able to transcribe the brainstorm ideas plus the dot totals into Excel, then adding the cluster titles as a separate column is fairly easy. The output can then be automatically sorted and displayed in various ways, e.g. by cluster then by priority, providing enhanced visibility and usefulness.

GALLERY WALK AND ISSUE CAPTURE

This is a workshop technique used in the middle and latter stages of a strategy process when significant analysis has already been carried out, and a large team needs to review, refine and consolidate the work carried out so far. This works well in aggregation and finalisation workshops (but is not generally appropriate in pilot workshops). It involves creating a 'gallery walk' – a structured display of the input data on wall-charts positioned around the workshop room – which the team systematically reviews to identify gaps and issues.

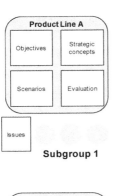

Subgroup 1

Subgroup 4

Participants
- Team splits into 4 groups which meet at each of 4 stations where 4 product line strategies are displayed on large charts.
- A representative from the product line presents the strategy in 20 minutes, followed by 10 minutes discussion / issue capture.
- Issues requiring resolution are captured on a blank flipchart next to the display.
- The teams move on to the next station but the product line representative stays at the station to repeat the presentation, and to capture any additional issues.
- The subgroups move on twice more so that each group gets 30 mins at each station.

Ideal Application
- Large groups for aggregation or finalisation.

Duration
- 30 mins x 4 = 2 hours

Strategy Leader
- Pre-defines the common structure for each strategy display.
- Briefs and coaches the product line representatives regarding their presentations and issue capture.
- Acts as time keeper to maintain adherence to 20 mins presentation plus 10 mins of issue capture.
- Rotates around the groups to support each team and ensure consistency.

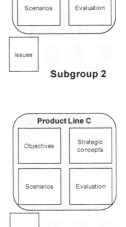

Subgroup 2

Subgroup 3

How it works

The gallery walk technique is typically used at the start of aggregation or finalisation workshops as a way of quickly and effectively communicating the draft strategies already created by the various pilots. The aim is to review and consolidate the various inputs, and identify issues for resolution. A typical structure for a gallery walk is illustrated on the previous page. This involves displaying four separate pilot strategies on wall-charts against four stations around a large room, and splitting a large group into four small sub-groups. Each sub-group gets 30 minutes at each station to review the strategies and capture issues on a flipchart. A pilot study representative mans each station, presents the strategy, and captures the issues. After each set time, the sub-groups move onto the next station to review the next strategy and add to the issues list. The presenters stay at the station and repeat the presentation four times.

The key role of the strategy leader is to guide the pilot study representatives regarding their presentations and issue capture activities. Templates for the strategies have been pre-defined in earlier workshops to ensure consistency of content. Timekeeping is essential and the presenters need to have rehearsed to ensure 20 minutes delivery. Discussion and issue capture is necessarily open and informal. The strategy leader is advised to rotate around the groups to ensure timely progress and effective issue capture.

Dot Prioritisation following a Gallery Walk

It is ideal to combine the gallery walk with a dot prioritisation immediately after the last presentation. This follows the usual process (see previous section) with each participant getting, say, 8 dots which they allocate to the 8 most important issues for resolution (across all four stations). The strategy leader then counts up the dots and writes the totals next to each issue.

CASE STUDY – Global Production Strategy

The gallery walk technique was used at the beginning of the aggregation and finalisation workshops in the *Global Production Strategy* project. This process allowed a large group to review, challenge and improve a huge amount of prepared material covering draft strategies for the respective global product lines and regional operations. This led to a strong foundation of common understanding within the team which, in turn, supported ongoing creative activity in enhancing the strategies and developing implementation plans.

Typical Duration

120 mins

A gallery walk covering 4 stations typically takes 120 minutes (30 minutes per station). Add another 30 minutes to cover a dot prioritisation.

Advantages	Disadvantages
• The key advantage of the gallery walk technique is that it supports intimate and meaningful review and discussion of large quantities of input data with large groups of stakeholders. This is achieved by splitting both the data and the group into more manageable chunks. • This is far better than the obvious alternative – a series of PowerPoint presentations delivered in plenary to the combined group. The problem with this is that it gets sterile very quickly, and discussion and issue capture is very difficult to manage effectively.	• The one possible disadvantage of this approach is that not everyone gets to hear all points of discussion directly. All participants get the chance to review all the issues captured, but the discussion behind each issue is, by definition, only heard by the sub-group directly involved. • This approach does not work well in smaller groups. It needs at least 15 participants with minimum 3 stations (i.e. 4 per sub-group plus 3 presenters) or the sub-groups do not have sufficient critical mass.

Ideal application

Gallery walk, issue capture and dot prioritisation work perfectly as a set of activities at the beginning of aggregation and finalisation workshops to review large amounts of input data. The gallery walk and issue capture technique requires a minimum of 15 participants (including presenters) and works best in large groups representing different businesses, functions or regions within a complex matrix organisation.

Practical Tips – Leading Gallery Walk and Issue Capture Sessions

137 **Take care in establishing common input templates**
Agree the templates with each of the teams preparing input data for the aggregation or finalisation stages. The better designed the templates, the higher the quality of communication in the gallery walk.

138 **Use charts and pictures rather than extended lists or bullet points**
'A picture paints a thousand words' in the context of a gallery walk. There is limited time to get across a significant amount of detail. This requires graphical creativity.

139 **Review and rehearse the input materials with the presenters**
This is worth doing, either in person or by teleconference, to fine tune all the inputs and to ensure consistency.

140 **Nurture a sense of competition between the presenters**
Share the inputs with the presenters to create a constructively competitive dynamic. Senior managers do not like looking unprepared and will raise each other's game.

141 **Plan preparation time to get the charts ready and to brief the presenters**
This may take up to an hour and is best completed before the other attendees turn up, impatient to get started. Kicking off a major strategy workshop is ideally not done in a fluster while sticking charts on walls!

142 **Spend a few mins with each group to check they are on the right track**
This means 3 minutes in each group during the presenting phase, then 3 minutes during the issue capture stage.

143 **Capture the issues quickly with minimum discussion**
The natural tendency will be to discuss and resolve issues but there is time for this later in the workshop. The presenter's job here is to clarify and qualify issues raised, record them accurately, and then move on.

144 **Explain the latest issues list with each new group**
This needs to happen *after* the presentation and *before* discussing additional issues. This is a cumulative process where each sub-group builds on the preceding efforts.

145 **Give clear guidance on timekeeping**
Give a 5 min then a 1 min warning before the end of each issue capture session.

146 **Shepherd the sub-groups quickly to the next station at changeover times**
This process works best with a high level of intensity and focus.

147 **Quickly review each issues list with the whole group before prioritising**
This helps everyone to properly register all the ideas before they are asked to prioritise.

WEIGHTED CRITERIA SCORING

This is the classic evaluation tool used for comparing strategic options or scenarios. It is a great way to balance the effect of a complex mix of factors on strategic decisions. It typically involves quantitative and qualitative factors and relies heavily on the expert judgement of the contributors. It is important to capture the rationale behind the scores as this can help to uncover deep insights regarding the strategic drivers.

Criteria	Weighting	Multi-room system	Lifestyle services	Technology licensing	iPod dock	Web-based services	Turntable	Wireless speakers	Music centre
·Profit margin	15.0%	5	5	5	4	2	3	2	1
·Total size of market	10.0%	5	3	1	2	2	2	2	3
·Benign competitive dynamic	12.5%	2	4	5	2	4	1	1	3
·Fit with long-term vision	12.5%	3	3	3	2	4	1	1	3
·Fit with competences	15.0%	4	4	3	4	4	4	4	2
·Low development costs	7.5%	5	4	2	2	2	4	4	3
·Quick development time	15.0%	5	3	2	4	2	4	3	2
·Low technical risk	12.5%	4	4	5	4	3	3	4	3
TOTAL	100.0%	4.1	3.8	3.4	3.2	2.9	2.8	2.6	2.4

How it works

A typical weighted criteria scoring (WCS) matrix is illustrated above. This involves setting up a simple spreadsheet with the rows listing meaningful criteria for comparison, and the columns representing each option or scenario. The process involves scoring each option against each criterion (often on a scale of 1 to 5). The criteria are weighted by allocating a percentage (i.e. their relative impact compared to the whole list of criteria) and a simple calculation and summation reveals total weighted scores for each option.

CASE STUDY – Technology Strategy

The illustration on the previous page is taken from the *Technology Strategy* project. To recap, this project was carried out with a specialist audio equipment supplier with around $30m annual turnover and 200 staff. The aim of the project was to develop a 3-year plan for R&D investment in new product and service offerings. The project format involved a workshop team of 12 cross-functional representatives with a 2-day pilot workshop followed by a 1-day finalisation workshop four weeks later. The pilot workshop involved various stages of brainstorming and simple prioritisation resulting in a shortlist of 8 strategic options. These were then investigated and defined in more detail against pre-defined templates via a break-out brainstorm process. This sequence of activities resulted in eight qualified strategic options with an initial level of detail regarding definitions and value propositions. This was now the perfect opportunity to conduct a WCS session to compare these options and to develop an understanding of the underlying strategic rationale and priorities.

The WCS spreadsheet illustrated has the 8 options as columns, and the 8 scoring criteria as rows. The session was facilitated by the strategy leader to capture the collective judgement of the workshop participants. Each option was scored against each criterion quickly and systematically. The strategy leader acted as mediator, helping the participants to agree each score. In addition, the strategy leader assisted the team in articulating the rationale for the scorings.

The result was to rank the options regarding attractiveness. In the chart the options have been arranged left-to-right in descending order of total score to show 'multi-room system' on the left as the most attractive option and 'music centre' on the right as the least attractive. This outcome provided guidance for validating analysis that was carried out after the workshop.

Weighted Criteria Scoring vs. Dot Prioritisation

WCS is clearly more sophisticated than dot prioritisation. However, it is still, in essence, a judgement-based tool and should not be presented as being particularly scientific. Hard data can be used to inform scoring on some of the more quantitative criteria e.g. total size of market. Despite its inherently qualitative nature, it does work remarkably well in helping to balance a complex mix of conflicting factors. It also tends to provoke high quality discussion and insights regarding the key issues and drivers. It is important, therefore, to capture notes regarding the drivers and the scoring rationale.

Typical Duration

90 mins

A WCS workshop session of the scope illustrated above (i.e. 8 options and 8 criteria) should take around 90 minutes. One feature of the process is that the scoring of all criteria for the first and second options tends to take disproportionately longer as the team gets comfortable with the process. Subsequent options can be done much more quickly. For this reason, covering 50% more options may only take 20% more time.

Advantages	Disadvantages
• The key advantage of WCS is its ability to compare strategic options or scenarios leading to 'directional' decisions.	• Whilst WCS is more sophisticated than dot prioritisation, it is still a judgement-based tool. It therefore relies on having the right mix of skills and experience in the team.
• This method balances a complex set of criteria, enabling the combination of both quantitative criteria (e.g. cost) and qualitative criteria (e.g. risk).	• With a large number of options, the process can become a bit mechanistic so it is important to keep discussion direct and to the point.
• The weighting approach balances the effect of potentially conflicting criteria e.g. if a highly profitable option is also high risk, then the total scoring is reduced accordingly. Conventional financial analysis may not incorporate these non-quantifiable factors.	• This method is not suitable for comparing very large quantities of options due to the time taken for discussion and reaching consensus on the scores. These can be reduced by dot prioritisation and clustering before conducting WCS.

Ideal application

Weighted criteria scoring is often used in pilot and aggregation workshops for comparing manageable sets of options or scenarios. It should not be used on large numbers of ideas (e.g. after formal brainstorms) without using dot prioritisation and clustering as a first-stage filter.

	Practical Tips – Leading Weighted Criteria Scoring Sessions
148	**Pre-define the proposed criteria and weightings** This will ensure a quick start, then you can allow the participants to refine as necessary.
149	**Check the template with senior stakeholders before the workshop** This tests your assumptions, allows refinements, and starts to build ownership.
150	**Get the team to refine the criteria and weightings during the workshop** Further iterations will fine tune the criteria and weightings and will secure ownership.
151	**Run the session live in Excel projected on the screen** Showing the results emerging live provides a focus for discussion and a bit of theatre.
152	**Start the process by scoring 1 option against all criteria as a pilot run** This tests each criterion and provides a total score that can be sanity-checked.
153	**Issue a 'guide sheet' to each participant with definitions of each criterion** This is not essential if the criteria are intuitive but helps if some criteria are more complex. This guide-sheet can also define calibration points for the scoring range.
154	**After the first option is complete, rate by criterion across all options** The first complete scoring of an option tests the criteria and yields a result for sanity-checking. The following runs across options by criterion allow direct comparison against each criterion. This approach makes the rating process easier and quicker.
155	**Make sure that the team uses the full range of scores available** Often teams score everything between 2 and 4 on a scale of 1 to 5. This makes the end scores too even. Make sure at least some options are scored 1 and 5.
156	**Allow some discussion, suggest a score, then test for possible consensus** Keep the process moving and lead if necessary. Don't let discussion go on too long or the process will get stale.
157	**Don't worry if one individual starts to take the lead on suggesting scores** This means you intervene less, and they own the outcome more. The consensus process only starts when someone makes a bid and is challenged to back it up.
158	**Capture the rationales for the scores** This is as important as the score itself. Capture a short description in a 'notes' column on the Excel matrix.
159	**At the end, sort the options by total score into descending order** This helps to accentuate the result and supports an overall sanity-check. This may then provoke more discussion and rescoring of items that do not look right.

2x2 MATRICES / BUBBLE CHARTS

2x2 matrices are excellent visualisation tools. These build on the weighted criteria scoring approach to provide a graphical output in two dimensions. Often the quadrants of the matrix align with a useful logic which can assist strategic decision-making. A bubble chart adds a third dimension (the size of the bubble) and enhances the usefulness of the output.

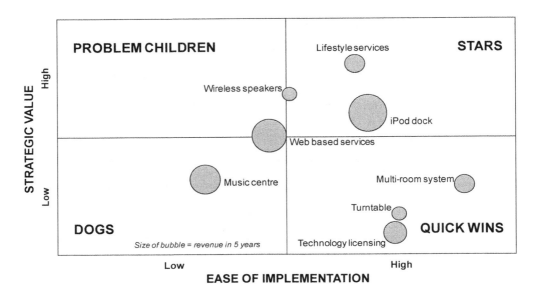

Overview

The illustration above shows a typical 2x2 matrix / bubble chart. The two x–y dimensions are 'strategic value' and 'ease of implementation'. The size of the bubble is 'revenue in 5 years'.

The classic 2x2 matrix / bubble chart

The example shown on the previous page is a typical 2x2 matrix / bubble chart which assesses a set of strategic options (taken from the *Technology Strategy* project). This scores the options against the two dimensions of a 2x2 matrix (strategic value vs. ease of implementation) thus positioning each option on the x–y axes. The size of the bubble is the estimated revenue in 5 years' time as a 'critical success factor'. The four quadrants of the 2x2 matrix are labelled to represent different types of strategic options. Hence the items with high value that are easy to implement (top right) are 'stars', high value but difficult are 'problem children' (top left), low value but easy are 'quick wins' (bottom right), low value and difficult are 'dogs' (bottom left). This classic 2x2 matrix / bubble chart provides a compelling visual output in a workshop. This example demonstrates clearly that, whilst the 'music centre' option has high revenue impact, it is actually potentially troublesome to implement. The best options here are the 'lifestyle services' and 'iPod dock' options which are easy to implement, and have good revenue impact.

Note: this format is just one option – there are an endless number of different 2x2 matrices which have different dimensions, different quadrant characterisations and niche applications.

STRATEGIC VALUE	Weighting	iPod dock	Turntable	Web-based services	Technology licensing	Lifestyle services	Wireless speakers	Music centre	Multi-room system
·Profit margin	30%	4	3	2	5	5	2	1	2
·Total size of market	20%	2	2	2	1	3	2	3	2
·Benign competitive dynamic	25%	2	1	4	5	4	1	3	2
·Fit with long-term vision	25%	5	1	4	3	3	1	3	3
TOTAL	100%	3.35	1.8	3	3.7	3.85	1.5	2.4	2.25

EASE OF IMPLEMENTATION									
·Fit with competences	30%	4	4	4	3	4	4	2	4
·Low development costs	15%	2	4	2	2	4	4	3	5
·Quick development time	30%	4	4	2	2	3	3	2	5
·Low technical risk	25%	4	3	3	5	4	4	3	4
TOTAL	100%	3.7	3.75	2.85	3.05	3.7	3.7	2.4	4.45

Approx revenue in £m/yr in 5 years									
		0.5	0.08	0.5	0.1	0.15	0.25	0.5	0.1

The underlying data (based on weighted criteria scoring)

The spreadsheet above shows the data behind the chart. This shows the two independent dimensions – 'strategic value' and 'ease of implementation' which are each broken down into four key criteria against which each option is scored on a range of 1–5. This is, in essence, two weighted criteria scoring matrices, one on top of the other. The calculated totals for 'strategic value' and 'ease of implementation' allow the plotting of the x–y graph for the 2x2 matrix.

The third dimension (which decides the size of the bubble on the chart) is 'approx revenue in £m/yr in 5 years' and is shown as the bottom row of data.

How it works

The workshop process to create a 2x2 matrix / bubble chart is similar to the weighted criteria scoring approach. The strategy leader mediates group discussion aimed at agreeing scores for each criterion for each strategic option. Once all the scores are completed, the graphical output can be displayed and used to clarify further strategic insights.

TOP TIP
If you intend to fill out a 2x2 matrix or bubble chart 'live' within a workshop, make sure that you have thoroughly tested and calibrated the Excel spreadsheet in advance. As the saying goes, 'Never do live TV with animals or children ... or untested Excel!'

Typical Duration

120 mins	The duration of a workshop session to create a 2x2 matrix / bubble chart is around 120 minutes. Scoring the first one or two options takes most time with the remainder completed much more quickly.

Advantages	Disadvantages
• The really important benefit of the 2x2 matrix / bubble chart approach is the graphical output. As a visualisation tool, this is difficult to beat. • This also provides an excellent 'killer slide' to go into the workshop report for communicating the outputs to other stakeholders. • All the advantages of the weighted criteria scoring approach apply here also – in particular, it helps to balance quantitative and qualitative criteria that are complex and conflicting.	• The main disadvantage of the 2x2 matrix is that, because it is over-used by consultants, it can be seen as a gimmick. • This means that it should only be used when the conceptual logic behind the key dimensions and the quadrant characterisations genuinely fit the central strategic question being investigated. • The possible disadvantages of the WCS approach described previously apply here also. In particular, because this is essentially a judgement-based tool, it requires the right mix of participants to work effectively.

Ideal application

2x2 matrices / bubble charts work best in helping to evaluate and compare a small number of strategic options or scenarios during pilot and aggregation workshops. The outputs often provide the basis for prioritising further validation analysis and for making preliminary strategic decisions.

Practical Tips – Leading 2x2 Matrix / Bubble Chart Sessions (mostly as for WCS)

160 **Pre-define the proposed criteria and weightings**
This will ensure a quick start, then you can allow the participants to refine as necessary.

161 **Check the template with senior stakeholders before the workshop**
This tests your assumptions, allows refinements, and starts to build ownership.

162 **Get the team to refine the criteria and weightings during the workshop**
Further iterations will fine tune the criteria and weightings and will secure ownership.

163 **Run the session live in Excel projected on the screen**
Showing the results emerging live provides a focus for discussion and a bit of theatre.

164 **Start the process by scoring 1 option against all criteria as a pilot run**
This tests each criterion and provides a total score that can be sanity-checked.

165 **Issue a 'guide sheet' to each participant with definitions of each criterion**
This is not essential if the criteria are intuitive but helps if some criteria are more complex.
This guide-sheet can also define calibration points for the scoring range.

166 **After the first option is complete, rate by criterion across all options**
The first complete scoring of an option tests the criteria and yields a result for sanity-checking. The following runs across options by criterion allow direct comparison against each criterion. This approach makes the rating process easier and quicker.

167 **Make sure that the team uses the full range of scores available**
Often teams score everything between 2 and 4 on a scale of 1 to 5. This makes the end scores too even.

168 **Allow some discussion, suggest a score, then test for possible consensus**
Keep the process moving and lead if necessary. Don't let discussion go on too long or the process will get stale.

169 **Don't worry if one individual starts to take the lead on suggesting scores**
This means you intervene less, and they own the outcome more. The consensus process only starts when someone makes a bid and is challenged to back it up.

170 **Capture the rationales for the scores**
This is as important as the score itself. Capture a short description in a 'notes' column on the Excel matrix.

171 **At the end, display the 2x2 matrix / bubble chart output**
This provides a compelling visual output, and provokes more discussion about the underlying strategic issues and drivers.

TRAFFIC LIGHT ANALYSIS

This is a simple and intuitive technique used for evaluating strategic options or projects at three levels – red/amber/green (hence the traffic light analogy). This works well in helping to rank qualitative judgements and it provides an effective visual output. It works best alongside conventional quantitative evaluation methods (such as discounted cash-flow analysis). As such, it is a useful complementary technique to financial evaluation (but is not normally used by itself).

	DCF Financial Analysis			Traffic Light Risk Analysis			
	NPV ($m)	IRR (%)	Payback (years)	Competitor reaction	Substitute technology	Technical challenge	Skills deficiency
iPod dock	22.3	18.1	2.3	Red		Amber	Amber
Turntable	12.1	9.2	4.2				Amber
Web-based services	8.6	25.1	1.2	Amber	Red	Amber	Amber
Technology licensing	5.2	33.2	0.8				
Lifestyle services	7.3	8.7	5.1	Amber	Red	Amber	Red
Wireless speakers	24.1	17.1	2.4	Red	Red	Amber	Amber
Music centre	13.2	11.2	4.1	Amber		Amber	
Multi-room system	26.3	37.1	1.8	Amber	Red	Amber	Amber

- Red
- Amber
- Green

How it works

Traffic light analysis works well in workshops to complement traditional discounted cash-flow (DCF) analysis as it introduces complementary qualitative factors. The DCF analysis is best done in advance of the workshop by qualified financial analysts but the traffic light analysis relies on the collective judgement of a set of experts and is best carried out within a workshop context.

CASE STUDY – **Technology Strategy**

The Technology Strategy project is used again as a case illustration to follow on from the weighted criteria scoring and 2x2 matrix descriptions earlier in this section. This project involved the creation of a set of alternative strategic options for developing new products and services to secure the long-term competitiveness of a small, specialist audio equipment company.

The output of a traffic light risk analysis coupled with DCF analysis for such a project is shown on the previous page. This shows the various strategic options for new products and services together with the DCF analysis and traffic light risk analysis. The DCF analysis provides the standard financial measures for each option in terms of net present value (NPV), internal rate of return (IRR) and payback. The traffic light risk analysis complements this with qualitative assessment of four key risk areas associated with implementation:

   a.   *competitor reaction* – the risk of adverse reaction by competitors resulting from market launch;
   b.   *substitute technology* – the risk of disruptive technologies replacing the need for this product;
   c.   *technical challenge* – the degree of perceived technical difficulty in developing the new product;
   d.   *skills deficiency* – the risk that the required skills fall outside the current capabilities.

These are typical examples of qualitative measures that might be used and these should be tailored to fit every individual project context.

The overall effect of the DCF analysis combined with the traffic light analysis gives the best of both worlds: quantitative assessment (based on robust financial analysis) plus qualitative assessment (capturing the experience and wisdom of the main stakeholders).

TOP TIP

You don't always need to do a full DCF model to get a good comparison of the business cases for different strategic options. Rough estimates of one-off investment, annual savings and simple payback, alongside traffic light analysis of qualitative factors, is extremely effective in strategy workshops.

Typical Duration

60 mins	The time required for a traffic light analysis of the scope illustrated above (i.e. 8 strategic options evaluated against 4 risk factors) is around 60 minutes. As with the other criteria-based evaluation methods, the first pass tends to take longer than the repeated passes so more options can be covered relatively quickly.

Advantages	Disadvantages
• The distinctive advantage of the traffic light method is the intuitive, visual output. Red, amber and green are instantly and universally understood. • The implied analogy of driving forward to the traffic lights fits well with the 'forward motion' sense of strategic development. • Traffic light analysis works best as a qualitative complement to quantitative analysis (particularly alongside DCF analysis on individual project options).	• Traffic light analysis can sometimes come across as overly simplistic. This is why it works best alongside quantitative measures and should not usually be used on its own. • By definition, traffic light analysis obviously only has three rating choices (red, amber or green). This implies rough approximation which, whilst it often fits well in workshop type activities, is not detailed enough for more accurate evaluation.

Ideal application

Weighted criteria scoring, 2x2 matrices, bubble charts and traffic light analysis are all variants on a theme and each has its niche application. All are appropriate for 'secondary' evaluation stages in a pilot workshop against a small number of strategic options or projects (where a 'primary' evaluation tool such as dot prioritisation has been used to condense the possibilities). The particular niche of traffic light analysis is to rate qualitative measures to complement quantitative measures (which have been provided separately by conventional approaches such as DCF analysis).

	Practical Tips – Leading Traffic Light Analysis Sessions
172	**Pre-define the evaluation criteria and check them with senior participants** This tests your assumptions, allows refinements, and starts to build ownership.
173	**Allow the workshop team to refine the criteria during the workshop** Further iterations will fine tune the criteria definitions and will secure ownership.
174	**Use Excel with conditional formatting for displaying red/amber/green** The simplest Excel method is to link the conditional formatting to the letters R, A and G.
175	**Run the session live in Excel projected on the screen** This is crucial as it provides a focus for discussion (everyone knows exactly what is being talked about at every moment). Showing the results emerging in real time provides a bit of theatre.
176	**Start the evaluation process by scoring one option against all criteria** This is worth doing to test that the process works properly and then you can sanity-check with the team whether the criteria are working and whether the output looks about right.
177	**Issue a 'guide sheet' defining the criteria and colour choice guidelines** The criteria definitions help maintain a common understanding of what is being assessed. The colour guide enables consistent scoring of red, amber and green.
178	**After the first option is complete, rate by criterion across all options** The first complete scoring of an option tests the criteria and yields a result for sanity-checking. The following runs across options by criterion allow direct comparison against each criterion. This approach makes the rating process easier and quicker.
179	**Capture the rationales for the colour rating** This is as important as the rating itself. Capture a short description in a 'notes' column on the Excel matrix.
180	**Review previous ratings if new discussion implies a change in rationale** This quite often happens and it is worth asking the team to re-score certain items if something learnt later in the process requires this.

TOP TIP

Conduct risk analysis using the traffic light method to uncover the worst fears of the most negative team members. This helps to disperse natural tensions.

F

SEVEN WORKSHOP ESSENTIALS

Room Layouts
Equipment and Materials
Choosing the Venue
Participation Guidelines
The Right Number of Participants
Summarising Techniques
Negotiating Points of Tension

ROOM LAYOUTS

Matching the room layout to the different types of workshop activity can have a radical impact on the success of each session. Room layouts provide a physical infrastructure that can help or hinder the various workshop processes of communication, creativity, evaluation, decision-making and task allocation. This section presents the sensible options and provides a simple guide of which layout to use when.

	U-shape	Boardroom	Cabaret	Standing up	Classroom
Works well with	Large groups Plenary sessions	Small groups Break-out sessions	Large groups Informal sessions	Large groups Informal sessions	Formal sessions
Type of activity	Structured communication	Structured creativity & evaluation	Semi-structured creativity Informal presentations	Semi-structured evaluation	Teaching
Ideal use	Briefings Formal brainstorms Structured evaluation Formal feedbacks	Break-out evaluation sessions	Break-out brainstorms Evening speakers	Dot prioritisation Clustering Gallery walks Carousel brainstorms	Not recommended for strategy workshops!

The range of sensible options

The diagram above summarises the main layout options for workshops, namely *U-shaped, Boardroom, Cabaret, 'Standing up'* and *Classroom*. The key variables to consider in choosing the best layout are the size of the group and the nature of the activity. For example, larger groups do not usually fit a boardroom style due to the physical limitations of a rectangular table so a U-shape or other arrangement is required. The five options are presented in more detail below.

Room Layouts – Key Options

U-shaped

This works well for large groups in supporting structured communications. The advantage of the open U-shape is that it is easier for participants to face each other and this promotes interactive discussion. This contrasts with the *Classroom* layout which limits interactivity and tends to channel communication through the strategy leader. One useful technique for strategy leaders using the U-shaped format is to move within the U to help link the team. This layout tends to be suited for briefings, formal brainstorms, structured evaluation (such as weighted criteria scoring) and mutual feedback of break-out groups' outputs.

Boardroom

Boardroom-style works well in small break-out groups for structured creativity sessions (such as option or scenario development). Here the participants face each other across a table which promotes intimate, in-depth discussions. This layout is not suitable for large groups as it feels too 'spread out' and communications from one end of the table to the other can be difficult.

Cabaret

This is a more informal layout and can work well with large groups to help create a more fun and dynamic atmosphere. This is also suitable for break-out brainstorms where each group works in isolation and then the various outputs are combined on a single wall-chart for the combined group to review. It also works well for evening guest speaker events where a more informal atmosphere is fitting.

Standing up

It is helpful to conduct certain workshop activities physically standing up around wall-charts or flipcharts. This works extremely well for semi-structured evaluation activities such as dot prioritisation, clustering, gallery walks and carousel brainstorms. The physical action of standing up refreshes the workshop dynamic and promotes interactivity. It does not work so well for structured communication and evaluation tasks where a more focused dynamic is required.

Classroom

This layout is only included as an example of one that does *not* work well in strategy workshops and is not recommended. This arrangement is too rigid for interactive strategy development amongst senior teams. Participants are facing each other's backs or cannot see each other at all. Communication tends to be channelled through the strategy leader rather than between the participants. This should be left to the school environment or for formal teaching activities.

EQUIPMENT AND MATERIALS

Selecting the right equipment and materials to support workshops may seem like a trivial matter until you find that something does not work as intended. Minor issues may just interrupt the flow of a workshop but more serious issues may significantly impact the constructive dynamic between strategy leader and participants by impairing common understanding or reducing visibility of the outputs. This section presents the key items that are important to get right.

Visualisation techniques are effectively useless if the content cannot easily be read

Key items that impact workshops

The fundamental piece of workshop equipment is, of course, the PC projector (or 'beamer'), without which the workshop simply could not function. Other critical items include wall-charts, post-its, pens and self-adhesive dots. Why these are important, and how best to use them, is described below.

Equipment and Materials – Key Items

PC projectors (or beamers)

The 'beamer' is the fundamental crutch for the workshop strategy leader. It takes a central role in providing a focus for most of the communication with the combined group, and will often provide the same role in break-out sessions. It is used for briefings, structured creativity (such as option or scenario development) and structured evaluation (such as weighted criteria scoring). Its great advantage is that it provides visibility of the strategic frameworks as they develop, helping to build common understanding and depth of insight. The outputs are infinitely adaptable and only limited by the power of the laptop and the creativity of the user. It is clearly a 'given' for any serious workshop activity and is so important that a back-up or contingency should be planned in case of equipment failure.

Wall-charts

Wall-charts are not as flexible as PowerPoint or Excel projected on a beamer but they have distinctive advantages and niche applications. The key advantage of wall-charts is that they are *constantly* visible through the course of a workshop (as opposed to PowerPoint slides or Excel spreadsheets which can obviously only be beamed on the wall one at a time). This feature allows the building of a cumulative output during a workshop which is continuously visible. This tangible, emerging story can be very appealing to the participants and also helps to assimilate and join up large quantities of complex outputs. Wall-charts tend to be used for the more informal creative activities such as brainstorming but also work well with structured creativity such as option or scenario development. Brainstorming wall-charts are often very large (maybe 2m high by 4m wide or 8 flipchart sheets) in order to capture the volumes of ideas emerging from exhaustive brainstorming. Option or scenario wall-charts are often flipchart size. Pre-printing large wall-charts incorporating a guiding framework can look impressive and comes across as clear and professional. Hand-drawn frameworks also work and can be constructed very quickly on-the-run or in breaks.

TOP TIP

Make sure in advance that the workshop room has at least one clear wall suitable for mounting wall-charts (if not, arrange to have a large portable notice board).

Equipment and Materials – Key Items

Post-its

If wall-charts are being used, there are really only two options for populating them: writing directly on the wall-chart or using post-its. In most cases, post-its are better. The obvious advantages are that they are easily moved and easily modified (i.e. discarded and replaced). The more subtle advantage is that they can help to promote clarity and brevity in the ideas and concepts developed by the workshop participants (simply by physically limiting how much detail can be written). This does require some guidance from the strategy leader to get the right level of detail.

| Develop green products | Develop green products e.g. energy efficient lightbulbs, sensor switches & rechargeable batteries | Develop a compelling range of green products including energy efficient lightbulbs, sensor switches and rechargeable batteries to meet the growing need for reduced carbon footprint |

Too vague   *About right*   *Too wordy*

As illustrated here, at one extreme (shown on the left) two or three words on a post-it can be vague and meaningless. At the other extreme (shown on the right), long sentences are difficult to digest and the text ends up too small to read. The optimum level (shown in the middle) is a short, descriptive sentence that captures the essence of an idea. This determines the ideal post-it size which, in most cases, is 5x3″ (or 127x76mm). The smaller option of 3x3″ (or 76x76mm) is just a bit too small.

Pens for post-it writing

Sounds trivial but getting the right type of pen is crucial and it is amazing how often this is overlooked. It is no good if, after all that inspiring, collective brainstorming effort, everyone is struggling to read what is displayed on the wall. The ideal pen is a medium-tip, permanent-ink, felt pen. This produces clear writing visible by a group of participants standing up or sitting down several feet away. Biro is too thin, flipchart markers are too thick.

Self-adhesive dots

The dot prioritisation method is a fundamental tool within the strategy leader's toolbox and this requires self-adhesive dots. Again, this may seem a trivial matter but this method just does not work with the wrong kind of dot! Size is the key issue. Generally these will be stuck on post-its in quantities of up to, say, 15 dots so if they are too big then they will obscure the writing. Too small and they are not visible enough or are too fiddly to handle. The ideal size is 8mm, which is a standard size available in most stationery stores.

CHOOSING THE VENUE

The choice of venue can have a significant impact on the dynamic of a workshop. The environment needs to align with the objectives and the spirit of the initiative. If you are looking for strategic thinking which is clear, creative, expansive and uncluttered then the facilities need to match.

Workshops are ideally held well away from the everyday pressures

Ideal aspects	Description
'Safe' and 'neutral'	The ideal venue for strategy workshops is off-site at a neutral facility where the participants can think creatively without the distractions of everyday pressures.
Light, airy and spacious	It helps if the main workshop rooms used are light, airy and spacious. This aids free thinking and helps avoid claustrophobia during moments of tension.
Inspiring setting	Views across beautiful open countryside are much more inspiring than views of the car park or the local gas works!
Accessible and practical	Don't go overboard on the setting. Minimise travel times and make sure that the venue has the facilities that senior managers require.
Evening events	Think about what you can do in the evenings as an informal opportunity to resolve issues and bond the team.

PARTICIPATION GUIDELINES

Providing some guidelines for what is expected of the participants in terms of their contribution to the workshop can help to set the right tone. This is especially helpful in cross-cultural situations where there may be different attitudes to hierarchy and to open challenge.

Setting the right tone

An open, empowered, non-hierarchical style is an intrinsic requirement of interactive strategy workshops and these are much less effective without it. The strategy leader sets the tone of the activity, and should therefore provide some simple guidelines during the initial workshop briefing. A set of typical guidelines is provided below. This should be tailored to the context and culture.

Sample guidelines

1. All participants are encouraged to be open and direct in imparting knowledge and in expressing opinions.
2. Be brief in your contributions and try to limit these to the most relevant and important issues.
3. Expect moments of tension and ambiguity – this is a natural part of the process.
4. We will aim for consensus but we are also happy to 'agree to disagree'.
5. Be prompt on start times and on returning from breaks.
6. Limit mobile phone and laptop usage to the formal breaks only.
7. Irresolvable issues will be recorded and the strategy leader will move the agenda on when we get bogged down.

THE RIGHT NUMBER OF PARTICIPANTS

Getting the numbers right for each type of workshop within the strategy development lifecycle can have a major impact on manageability. The main impact of numbers is the level of depth obtainable (depth is generally indirectly proportional to numbers). Below are some general 'rules of thumb' to use as guidance during workshop design.

Workshop	Range	Guiding rationale
Pilot workshop	6–12	Significant depth is required and this works best with between 6 and 12 participants. Less than 6 means that the required spread of inputs is not covered. More than 12 is difficult to manage with any depth.
Aggregation workshop	12–24	By definition, this needs to cover breadth as well as depth and the objective is to join up and enhance various inputs. Much of the depth has been developed in advance and this is workable with up to 24 participants. Less than 12 probably does not make sense as we need representation from different organisational entities (i.e. functions, regions, product lines etc).
Finalisation workshop	12–36	For this activity most of the depth has been covered and the focus is on fine-tuning and getting buy-in across multiple stakeholders. 36 wild cats are very difficult to manage but this is just about do-able with careful preparation. The classic technique of 'divide and conquer' should be used here i.e. frequent break-out activities with plenary session strictly limited for briefing and mutual feedback and not for any core creative or evaluation activities.
Break-out sessions	3–8	The size of break-out teams depends on the degree of structure provided. The more structured activities (such as option development or weighted criteria scoring) work well with up to 8 participants. Here the pre-defined structure helps to maintain cohesion and common understanding amongst a relatively large group. For less structured activities (such as break-out brainstorming) smaller numbers work better. Three is the minimum as one person in a pair can tend to dominate.

SUMMARISING TECHNIQUES

Summarising is a core competence required of strategy leaders. Strategy workshops are intense and cover significant detail. At any one point in time, some of the participants will be losing the plot. There is a regular need for the strategy leader to help the group stand back to see things in perspective. Below are some simple guidelines to assist.

	Practical Tips – Summarising Techniques
181	**Create space to reflect** Plan some space in the agenda for the strategy leader to step back and reflect. This may mean a coffee or meal break, or simply a few minutes where break-out groups can be left to self-manage.
182	**Answer the 'So what?' question** This is the question at the back of every impatient workshop participant's mind: 'we've had to go through all these contrived activities – so what – how will this help the business and how will it affect my part in it?' This means periodically going back to the objectives and the target deliverables and explaining where we are in our journey to achieving these.
183	**Create milestone updates** This might just mean a single set of bullets on a flipchart or a PowerPoint slide to capture the key points so far. The process of creating it will probably help structure and sharpen your own thinking. Presenting it will probably help get everyone back on the same page.
184	**Make use of evenings** The middle evenings between workshop days are the ideal opportunity to construct a synthesised summary of the workshop findings so far. Check this with some senior stakeholders in the bar. Present this first thing next morning to rally the troops.
185	**Create a summarising picture** This is easier said than done but worth attempting. A simple graphic that represents the essence of a strategy is an extremely powerful communications tool. This may take several iterations spanning several workshops but is worth the effort.

NEGOTIATING POINTS OF TENSION

Tension is a natural part of strategy workshops involving wild cats. Some might even argue that it is actually a pre-requisite for breakthrough thinking. It is therefore to be actively encouraged and orchestrated but this needs to be managed in a controlled fashion otherwise everything can start to unravel. Below are some guidelines.

	Practical Tips – Negotiating Points of Tension
186	**Plan cycles of tension build and release** As a general principle, creative activities build tension and evaluation activities help to release tension. This is because ambiguity and confusion tends to increase as we create more ideas and this can become mentally overpowering. Plan cycles of creativity and evaluation to manage tension.
187	**Monitor levels of tension** Be aware of the tell-tale signs of political tensions building in the group. The first sign is often deterioration in the quality of discussion, followed soon by participants defending their territory.
188	**Mediate during heated discussions** Intervene in heated discussions and try to build a compromise position. Two arguing wild cats often find they are more aligned than they think and simply re-articulating and summarising a key point demonstrates this.
189	**Call a 'time out'** If tensions persist, call a break and resolve tricky issues in a smaller group.
190	**Plan for time in the bar** Evening events such as informal dinners and time in the bar can often provide a natural opportunity to relieve simmering tensions. It is amazing how seemingly violent disagreements at the end of a long, hot day have been resolved by the next morning.

> *If we haven't experienced points of tension, we haven't tested our comfort zones and we haven't created breakthrough thinking.*
> Senior Vice President, Global Production Strategy

CONCLUSION

As international business cultures increasingly evolve towards decentralised, empowered organisational models, strategy workshops are set to become a permanent and central feature of the strategy development process. Politics will always be a key part of the backdrop, so the stakes will remain high. It will always be a challenge to blend facts, experience and gut-feel to create ambitious but practical strategies. The benefits of involving all the right stakeholders, in terms of relevance and ownership of the outcome, will continue to mean that the total-involvement approach is preferable to top-down decree or simply outsourcing strategy to external consultants. Running effective strategy workshops may have just become a critical success factor in 21st-century businesses.

There is, therefore, a strong need to define good practice in this area. It is hoped that this book has made a small impact by defining some guiding principles and contributing specific techniques and practical tips. These are not, of course, definitive guidelines and each strategy leader should choose what works for them and tailor each element to fit both their individual style and the project context. The core objective of this book, however, remains fixed: to assist strategy leaders in running workshops that inspire innovative strategy, motivate the team to make it happen, and remain long in the memory as game-changing events that transformed the business.

Appendix

190
PRACTICAL TIPS –
Checklist

Compilation of shorthand versions
from within the text

	Planning a Structured Journey of Discovery – see page 19
1	Involve all stakeholders at the outset to agree the project framework
2	Use workshops as focal points for creating and agreeing strategy
3	Use regular telephone meetings for project updates, not for workshops
4	Design the process to involve divergent then convergent thinking
5	Design the project to fit the project customer–supplier relationships
6	Hold pilot workshops early on in the process
7	Use pilot workshops to crystallise the strategy 'working proposition'
8	Do not apply formal analysis until after the strategic concepts are clear
9	Use the finalisation workshop to sign off the strategy and mobilise launch
	Herding Wild Cats – see page 24
10	Each cat has a unique natural environment where it feels at ease
11	Let the big cats regularly run free but don't cause a cat fight
12	Big cats need regular feeding with raw meat
13	Understand potential winners and losers early on and take action
14	Night time activities (i.e. in the bar) often disperse tensions
15	Take appropriate action to dissipate continuing tensions
	Engaging the Team via One-on-One Interviews – see page 32
16	Talk to each key contributor individually before the main team activities
17	Use telephone interviews for efficiency and intimacy
18	45 minutes per interview is about right
19	Use a short checklist of broad topics and an open questioning style
20	Find out what the interviewee thinks is important
21	Air time should be 80% interviewee, 20% interviewer
22	Circulate a summarised, anonymous digest of the key interview findings

	Getting the Right Level of Data – see page 37
23	Second guess the answer to help with data collection
24	Bundle up data needs and make the minimum individual requests
25	Make sure there is a clear purpose for all data collected
26	Data analysis should support strategic thinking, not lead it
27	Respect both the data-junkies and the data-phobes

	Ensuring Seamless Transition to Implementation – see page 45
28	Seed implementation champions into the strategy process
29	Dedicate 50% of the finalisation workshop to implementation planning
30	Identify clear accountability for each implementation project
31	Develop a sense of competition between implementation champions
32	Identify tangible incentives for delivery
33	Don't demobilise until the quick wins are secured

	Leading Pilot Workshops– see page 53
34	More doing than listening
35	More wall-charts than PowerPoint
36	Cover the walls with an emerging story
37	Get the team to spend time on its feet
38	Be wary of the 'So what?' question
39	Know the difference between 'exhaustive' and 'exhausting'
40	Everyone must contribute, no-one should dominate
41	Summarise after every major activity
42	Manage moments of tension and release
43	Use little bits of humour, fun and drama

	Leading Aggregation Workshops – see page 57
44	Meet the evening before for the briefing
45	Pre-define break-out teams where possible
46	Be careful to balance break-out teams
47	Look for opportunities to harmonise
48	Develop a new, common language via harmonisation
49	Simple is much harder than complex
50	Arrange an external speaker
51	Instil an increasing sense of urgency
52	Expect ongoing refinements and iteration
	Leading Finalisation Workshops – see page 61
53	Create simple, standard templates for all inputs
54	Have all the detail to hand as a back-up in an accessible form
55	Don't get lost in details
56	Invest in individual pre-briefings
57	Promote constructive tension and internal competition
58	Call special 'issue resolution' break-outs where required
59	Arrange a real customer to speak at the middle evening
60	Cross-check financials for consistency
61	Reinforce the short-term plan as well as the distant vision
	Leading Audit Workshops – see page 65
62	Choose the right timing
63	Make sure the audit 'champions' are well prepared
64	Celebrate the progress-to-date and any early wins
65	Prepare possible workstream titles in advance
66	Refine the workstream definitions again after Day 1
67	Smaller working groups sometimes require more coaching

	Leading Formal Brainstorms – see page 72
68	Make sure the key question is crystal clear
69	Ask for two minutes' private thought before kick-off
70	The outputs need to be visible to all participants at all times
71	The strategy leader should act as scribe
72	Clarify and simplify the idea descriptions when appropriate...
73	... but don't overdo it or the process will drag on
74	Call a further two minutes' private thought midway
75	Try to identify obvious gaps and challenge the participants to fill these
76	Keep it moving – don't allow things to get bogged down
77	When momentum recedes, ask for 2 more ideas then close the session
	Leading Break-out Brainstorms – see page 76
78	Prepare checklists for each sub-group as guidance on scope
79	Include the specific question being asked on the checklist
80	Make sure the capture of ideas on post-its is meaningful and legible
81	Consider nominating a leader for each sub-group
82	Keep the sub-groups in the same room
83	Check soon after launch that all groups are on the right track
84	Use a second coaching session to challenge and identify possible gaps
85	Make sure the wall-chart is the right size!
86	For the stage 2 review, keep discussion short and to the point
87	Get the originators of stage 2 ideas to record these on new post-its
88	Summarise the general themes emerging at the end of the session

	Leading Carousel Brainstorms – see page 80
89	Test your choice of themes with senior participants in advance
90	Plan a break directly before the session to prepare the room
91	Make sure that there is enough space in the room
92	Number off the participants to quickly identify random sub-groups
93	Make it clear this is quick-fire and ask for a final surge of energy
94	Start the first session like a race – ready, steady, go – with watch in hand
95	Check with each sub-group at kick-off to make sure that they are on track
96	Give a one-minute warning before the end of each rotation
97	Remind everyone to review the existing ideas after each rotation
98	Be a visible and audible presence in shepherding the process
	Leading Option/Scenario Development Sessions – see page 85
99	Get the right level of detail in the templates
100	Mix qualitative and quantitative elements in the template
101	Design break-out groups around the skills and champions available
102	Know when to have self-facilitating sub-groups
103	Use PowerPoint for facilitated sub-groups, wall-charts for self-facilitated
104	Expect the options or scenarios to evolve
105	Strictly limit mutual feedback time
106	Consider weighted criteria scoring as a next step
	Leading Storyboarding Sessions – see page 90
107	Pre-define the linkage between options/scenarios and the storyboard
108	Get the right level of detail
109	Mix qualitative and quantitative elements within the storyboard
110	Aim to have self-facilitating sub-groups
111	PowerPoint is marginally preferred over wall-charts for the templates
112	Capture any necessary changes to options and scenarios that emerge
113	Set different missions for each group to cover the full spectrum

	Leading Action Planning Sessions – see page 94
114	Check the foundation/enabling project titles with senior participants
115	Carefully design the break-out teams
116	Don't spend too long – this is still broad-brush planning
117	Create healthy competition between sub-groups on level of ambition
118	Rotate the 'internal customers' between the sub-groups to challenge
119	Make the preceding outputs available to each group for reference
120	PowerPoint is marginally preferred to wall-charts for the templates

	Leading Dot Prioritisation Sessions – see page 101
121	How to define the right number of dots per participant
122	Don't allow discussion or conferring
123	Make sure the participants have registered and absorbed all the ideas
124	Don't make this sound more sophisticated than it is
125	Use a coffee break to count up the dots and to prepare the result
126	Ask an assistant to capture the output straight away in Excel
127	Encourage consideration of other people's ideas (not just one's own)!

	Leading Clustering Sessions – see page 105
128	Make it clear that this is fairly rough but also a bit of fun
129	Don't be tempted to intervene too early
130	Observe closely and start to think of possible cluster titles
131	Intervene as soon as the emerging clusters are clear
132	Following the first intervention, become part of the team
133	Re-title clusters if necessary
134	Take editorial control towards the end of the process
135	Create a 'miscellaneous' cluster for the misfits
136	Consider documenting the result live in Excel

	Leading Gallery Walk and Issue Capture Sessions – see page 109
137	Take care in establishing common input templates
138	Use charts and pictures rather than extended lists or bullet points
139	Review and rehearse the input materials with the presenters
140	Nurture a sense of competition between the presenters
141	Plan preparation time to get the charts ready and to brief the presenters
142	Spend a few mins with each group to check they are on the right track
143	Capture the issues quickly with minimum discussion
144	Explain the latest issues list with each new group
145	Give clear guidance on timekeeping
146	Shepherd the sub-groups quickly to the next station at changeover times
147	Quickly review each issues list with the whole group before prioritising
	Leading Weighted Criteria Scoring Sessions – see page 113
148	Pre-define the proposed criteria and weightings
149	Check the template with senior stakeholders before the workshop
150	Allow the team to refine the criteria and weightings during the workshop
151	Run the session live in Excel projected on the screen
152	Start the process by scoring 1 option against all criteria as a pilot run
153	Issue a 'guide sheet' to each participant with definitions of each criterion
154	After the first option is complete, rate by criterion across all options
155	Make sure that the team uses the full range of scores available
156	Allow some discussion, suggest a score, then test for possible consensus
157	Don't worry if one individual starts to take the lead on suggesting scores
158	Capture the rationales for the scores
159	At the end, sort the options by total score into descending order

	Leading 2x2 Matrix / Bubble Chart Sessions – see page 118
160	Pre-define the proposed criteria and weightings
161	Check the template with senior stakeholders before the workshop
162	Allow the team to refine the criteria and weightings during the workshop
163	Run the session live in Excel projected on the screen
164	Start the process by scoring 1 option against all criteria as a pilot run
165	Issue a 'guide sheet' to each participant with definitions of each criterion
166	After the first option is complete, rate by criterion across all options
167	Make sure that the team uses the full range of scores available
168	Allow some discussion, suggest a score, then test for possible consensus
169	Don't worry if one individual starts to take the lead on suggesting scores
170	Capture the rationales for the scores
171	At the end, display the 2x2 matrix / bubble chart output
	Leading Traffic Light Analysis Sessions – see page 122
172	Pre-define the evaluation criteria and check them with senior participants
173	Allow the workshop team to refine the criteria during the workshop
174	Use Excel with conditional formatting for displaying red/amber/green
175	Run the session live in Excel projected on the screen
176	Start the evaluation process by scoring one option against all criteria
177	Issue a 'guide sheet' defining the criteria and colour choice guidelines
178	After the first option is complete, rate by criterion across all options
179	Capture the rationales for the colour rating
180	Review previous ratings if new discussion implies a change in rationale

	Summarising Techniques – see page 132
181	Create space to reflect
182	Answer the 'So what?' question
183	Create milestone updates
184	Make use of evenings
185	Create a summarising picture
	Negotiating Points of Tension – see page 133
186	Plan cycles of tension build and release
187	Monitor levels of tension
188	Mediate during heated discussions
189	Call a 'time out'
190	Plan for time in the bar

Index

About Strajectory

Strajectory helps businesses to realise their full potential through the creation of innovative and practical strategy. Our experienced strategy practitioners work with your senior management teams to identify and manage the critical projects that must be delivered to secure competitive advantage.

Working as a team

Strajectory delivers its services through team workshops, executive coaching and independent expert advice. Our experienced strategy practitioners work with your senior teams to:

- Listen... and understand your unique business context and culture
- Create tailored and innovative strategy development plans
- Apply the latest tools and techniques to enhance your management skills and processes
- Assist with 'light touch' support of strategy implementation.

Partnership

Strajectory develops long-term partnerships with our clients:

- Building a strengthening foundation of knowledge and relationships
- Adding increasing value over time.

By working this way, our team can demonstrate tangible improvements in your competitiveness and profitability so that our reputation speaks for itself.

For more details, please see *www.strajectory.co.uk*

Lightning Source UK Ltd.
Milton Keynes UK
UKOW07f0713231117
313215UK00005B/233/P